The Carolina Pirates

and

Colonial Commerce

1670–1740

The Reprint Company
Spartanburg, South Carolina

The Reprint Company
Post Office Box 5401
Spartanburg, South Carolina 29301

Reprinted: 1971
ISBN 0-87152-065-6
Library of Congress Catalog Card Number: 70-149345

Manufactured in the United States of America on long-life paper

V-VI-VII

THE CAROLINA PIRATES AND COLONIAL
COMMERCE, 1670-1740

JOHNS HOPKINS UNIVERSITY STUDIES

IN

HISTORICAL AND POLITICAL SCIENCE

HERBERT B. ADAMS, Editor

History is past Politics and Politics present History.—*Freeman*

TWELFTH SERIES

V-VI-VII

THE CAROLINA PIRATES AND COLONIAL COMMERCE, 1670–1740

BY

SHIRLEY CARTER HUGHSON

BALTIMORE
THE JOHNS HOPKINS PRESS
PUBLISHED MONTHLY
May-June-July, 1894

THE FRIEDENWALD CO., PRINTERS,
BALTIMORE.

INTRODUCTION.[1]

In the present work the author will attempt to present the results of a study of the pirates of the coasts of the two Carolinas during the seventeenth and eighteenth centuries. The purpose will be to show how they arose; how they were regarded by the colonists and the English authorities respectively; how they affected the life and commerce of those parts of the new world they frequented; and, finally, how they were exterminated.

From time immemorial the "odious and horrid" crime of piracy has been the subject of special and most severe laws in almost every country of Europe, and the people of England, always distinguished for their love of law and order, have from the earliest period regarded it with peculiar abhorrence. The ancient law of the realm dealt with it in a very specific manner. The pirate was declared a "hostis humani generis," and by the English law, both common and statutory, he was accorded no rights which any one was bound to respect. He was a common enemy to mankind, with whom neither faith nor oath was to be kept. "As therefore," says the old commentator, "he has renounced all the benefits of society and government, and has

[1] The author desires to thank the following gentlemen for advice and assistance in the preparation of this study: Professor H. B. Adams, Johns Hopkins University; Dr. Edward Eggleston, New York; Professor W. P. Trent, University of the South; Dr. S. B. Weeks, of Trinity College, N. C.; Mr. James Sprunt, British Vice-Consul, Wilmington, N. C.; General Edward McCrady, Ex-Mayor W. A. Courtenay, Mr. Daniel Ravenel, Major E. Willis, Mr. Yates Snowden, Mr. Julius Seabrook, all of Charleston; Mr. Henry L. Barker, Oakley, S. C. Also to Miss Helen V. Banskett for faithful researches made in the records in the Secretary of State's office, Columbia, S. C.

reduced himself afresh to the savage state of nature by declaring war against all mankind, all mankind must declare war against him, and every community hath a right by the rule of self-defense to inflict that punishment upon him which every individual would in a state of nature have been otherwise entitled to do for any invasion of his person or personal property."[1] Further than this, no person charged with piracy could claim the benefit of clergy or the right of sanctuary, and if the crime was attempted on the ocean, and the pirates be overcome, the captors were at liberty to hang them from the yard-arm " without any solemnity of condemnation." In all declarations of general pardon it was understood, even though no clause to that effect was inserted, that pirates were excepted. It was usually customary, however, to enter a clause stating this exception specifically.

According to the very early English law, piracy in a subject was a species of petty treason, but by an act of 25 Edward III., c. 2, it was made a felony, and since that time has always been classed as such.

It was on the common law, and numerous early English acts, that judicial proceedings against pirates were based, until by a statute of 28 Henry VIII. the law was fully set forth in an extensive act of Parliament, which defined clearly the crime of piracy with its numerous modifications, and appointed the method of trial, execution of sentence, etc. Up to this time all pirates had been tried in England before the Lord Admiral, but the preamble of this act set forth the difficulty of bringing prisoners from remote parts, and provincial Vice-Admiralty Courts, by which all cases under the jurisdiction of the Admiral could be tried, were established. It has been under this act, or modifications of it, that all subsequent trials have been held.

Some of the refinements of the pirate law which arose later were very remarkable and are worthy of notice. For instance, if an Englishman was captured from an alien war

---

[1] Blackstone, Book IV., Chap. 5.

vessel while England was engaged in war against the flag under which she was sailing, the prisoner was deemed a pirate and dealt with accordingly. Again, if an alien was taken in the act of serving on an English pirate against English shipping, and his country chanced to be at war with England at the time, the prisoner was adjudged to be engaged in legitimate hostilities and could be dealt with only by the military authorities.

At the time of the founding of the American colonies the English mind was absolutely set against piracy, and the severity of the law was founded in the same principle that underlies the severity of the law in many parts of the United States against larceny from the freehold. So peremptorily were cases disposed of that few defendants ever escaped the extreme penalty. If we can form any judgment from the reports of trials which have been handed down, in a great majority of cases, as in witchcraft, very little more than the mere preferment of the charge was needed to insure conviction. One of the most interesting phases we have to trace is how this sentiment changed, and how from abhorring piracy the English in America grew not only to tolerate but to encourage it.

The subject of piracy on the Carolina coasts divides itself into two periods: the first, from the founding of the colonies, 1660-70, to the end of the seventeenth century; and the second, from 1713 to 1719, or, to measure it by events, from the Peace of Utrecht, which threw many American privateers out of employment, to the downfall of the Proprietary government in South Carolina, when the colonial affairs were taken from the control of a trade corporation and passed into the strong hands of the king's officers.

In studying this or any other subject relating to the two Carolinas one is liable to constant confusion owing to the indiscriminate use of the name Carolina by the old authorities. It is used by nearly all the writers without any definition or qualification, and frequently when an occurrence is narrated it is well-nigh impossible to know to which of the later divisions of the province it should be referred.   In the present work the author has had this difficulty to contend with at every step, but he trusts that the careful verification of authorities he has made in every instance will save him from this rock upon which so many excellent historians have been stranded.

THE CAROLINA PIRATES AND COLONIAL COMMERCE, 1670-1740.

CHAPTER I.

The appearance of pirates on the Carolina coast was coeval with the earliest settlements in the New World. The first accounts date back to the year 1565, soon after the French colony under Ribault was planted near the site of the present town of Port Royal. In 1564 the French king, learning of the impoverished condition of the first settlement, sent out three relief ships under Laudonière, who carried with him adventurers from every part of France, who were induced to join the expedition by the accounts which were circulated of the marvellous wealth of the country. Arriving in Carolina, they found that the reports had been greatly exaggerated, and, discouraged at the prospect, they determined to try their fortunes by cruising as pirates in the West Indies. Laudonière refused to give them passports, whereupon a large number mutinied and forced him by imprisonment to comply with their demands. They then stole a vessel and set sail for the Spanish Main. At first they met with much success, and finally grew so bold as to run into Jamaica, terrorize the entire island, and round up the escapade by holding the Spanish governor a prisoner on board their ship. Having been defeated in an engagement with the Spaniards, however, the pilot, who had been forced to join them, steered back to Carolina, where Laudonière, who had in the meantime strengthened himself in the colony, had them arrested and condemned to execution for piracy as an "example to posterity." A strong address was delivered to the settlers on the enormity of the crime, after which the sentence was executed.[1]   The year following this occurrence the French colony was wiped out of existence by the Spaniards, and it was more than a hundred years before any further settlements were attempted in Carolina.

This instance was but an isolated one, however, and can scarcely be considered as a part of the piracies which enter so largely into the history of the early American colonies. At this time none of the English colonies of North America had been planted, and it was not until the founding of these that the famous piracies of the 17th and 18th centuries began.   From them the old buccaneers of the West Indies drew many of their most desperate companions, who in after-years assumed the leadership of expeditions never surpassed in the annals of piracy.   Very many of these early English settlers were adventurers,—not in the then honorable meaning of the term, but in the strictest latter-day disreputable sense.   The countries of Europe, when anxious to rid themselves of turbulent elements, offered special inducements to the objectionable individuals to emigrate.   By England particularly was this custom practiced, and the better classes in the colonies frequently complained of the unloading of the refuse population of the mother country on their shores.   One of the best accounts yet given of the colonization methods of the seventeenth century is by the historian Doyle.   " It became a trade," he says, " to furnish the plantations with servile labor drawn from the offscourings of the mother-country."   So far had this policy been adopted by the English government, that in 1661 " a committee was appointed to consider the best means of furnishing labor to the Plantations by authorizing contractors to transport criminals, beggars, and vagrants."   " Runaway apprentices," continues Doyle, " faithless husbands and

---

[1] Carroll's Collections, Vol. I., pp. liii-liv.

wives, fugitive thieves and murderers were thus enabled to escape beyond the reach of civil or criminal justice."[1]

But not only were the lowest criminal classes induced to emigrate, but on more than one occasion was it attempted to settle objectionable statesmen in the Plantations, while others, fearing to lose their heads at home, escaped the vengeance of the authorities by taking up a residence in some distant settlement. No less distinguished a personage than the great Earl of Shaftesbury, one of the original Lords Proprietors of Carolina, at one time sought to escape a threatened prosecution for his alleged treasonable leanings by fleeing to that colony.[2] It is thus seen that a large proportion of the first settlers of many parts of America were banished criminals of the lowest class, and in numbers of cases the leaders, while not really depraved characters, were at least agitators of a type whose presence would by no means conduce to the political health of any community. So anxious were the Proprietors of the various colonies to have their plantations settled that they adopted all kinds of schemes to secure this end.[3] In Carolina large bounties of land were offered to every settler who would bring with him a certain number of servants. It was easy enough for a new-comer to attach to himself any number of low characters, enter them as his servants, receive the broad domain to which he was entitled, and then either turn the people loose on the country, or else attempt to settle them as " leetmen " in accordance with the terms of the laws of the colony.[4] It was never practicable to enforce these terms of vassalage, and these rogues knew well enough what their freedom

---

[1] Doyle's English Colonies in America, Vol. I., pp. 383-84 (American edition). Also see Hewat's South Carolina in Carroll, Vol. I., p. 54 *et seq.* Also memorandum in S. C. Hist. Society Coll., Vol. I., p. 206, for notice of female convicts. Also Hawks' N. C., Vol. 2, p. 230 *et seq.*

[2] Cook's Hist. of Party, Vol. I., p. 210.

[3] In 2 S. C. Stats., p. 124, is published an act offering special inducements to delinquent French and English debtors to settle in South Carolina. The date of its passage is December 5th, 1696.

[4] See Fundamental Constitutions of Carolina.

would be in a new, wild country like America. The form
of government in many of the colonies, and especially in
Carolina under the Fundamental Constitutions of the ideal-
istic John Locke, was purely experimental, and as is the
case in all new countries, the law was but slightly regarded
because the power to enforce it was weak. Considering all
these circumstances it is not surprising that bold, bad men
with criminal propensities, if not genuine outlaws, should
flock to the American Plantations as a field in which they
could indulge their evil natures with comparatively little
interruption. This was the class that fostered the spirit that
needed but an opportunity to break out into every kind of
crime that occasion might suggest. And opportunity was
not wanting from the very moment they landed on the shores
of the New World.

It is safe to say that when the English, under the charter
of Charles II., settled Carolina, the pirates of the Spanish
Main had for many years been occupying the coast at their
own pleasure. Indented as it was by numerous harbors
and inlets, it afforded them a safe refuge when pursued by
enemies, and was a most available place for refitting and
repairing after a cruise. Here, too, they could bring their
prizes, and, if ancient tradition be true, bury their treasure.
The coast country was a wilderness inhabited only by
scattered tribes of savages, and once within the headlands of
the spacious harbors they were protected from interference
and could plot their nefarious schemes at their leisure.

Sir John Yeamans, of the Barbadoes, made a settlement
on the Cape Fear river in 1664, and Governor Sayle arrived with his commission from the Lords Proprietors in
1670, and made his first landing at Port Royal, near the site
of the French colony of the previous century. We have but
few records of the personnel of these pioneer parties, but
there can scarcely be any doubt that they included many persons who were not loth to make friends with the pirates.
Nor is it to be supposed that the pirates themselves were
anything but pleased at the settlement of the coast. It

simply afforded them new and convenient rendezvous, and they had nothing to fear from the authority of the Governors or their officers. Powerful as they were upon the sea, and carrying, in many cases, commissions from the English king, it was not to be expected that they would stand in very great awe of the young and struggling colonies, especially when, as has been shown, the men who were to constitute a large part of the settlements were in a general way in sympathy with the buccaneers in their criminal practices. The pirate chiefs simply looked upon the settlements as communities with which they could carry on a profitable trade, and from which they could, in many instances, recruit their forces. If the suspicions of the colonial governments were aroused, no proof of crime was forthcoming, and the pirates could still come and go among the people without fear of hindrance.

The most powerful of these pirates were men who had entered upon their careers with special commissions from the English government.[1] Ever since before Blake's great victory over the Spaniards at Santa Cruz in 1657, the American seas were covered with privateers commissioned to prey upon the commerce of Spain. Making the English colonies their headquarters, these bold adventurers would make sudden dashes on the coasts of the Spanish provinces, seize any vessels sailing under the colors of his Catholic Majesty, and return with their rich plunder long before any steps could be taken to avenge their depredations. For many years scarcely a month passed without seeing these licensed freebooters sail into Carolina, their vessels laden with the spoils of their latest expedition. Not infrequently they would meet with rich prizes, ships of treasure and plate, and on coming into the colony would scatter their gold and silver about with so generous a hand that their appearance soon came to be welcomed by the trading classes; and by means of their money they ingratiated themselves not only

---

[1] See Chalmers' Polit. Annals, Art. Carolina, p. 546.

with the people, but with the highest officials of the government. For many years after the founding of Carolina most of the currency in circulation was the gold and silver pieces brought in by the pirates and privateers from their cruises in the West Indian waters.[1] It is therefore not surprising that the colonists should have entertained sentiments of friendship for them, and the moral tone of the mass of the inhabitants was not so high that they were particularly shocked at certain rumors which obtained that the strangers did not always secure their rich prizes in a manner that could bear the light of an official inquiry.

When we consider the relations then existing between Spain and England in the New World, it is impossible to look upon this toleration and encouragement wholly in the light of a crime. The Spaniards of Havanna and Florida were in a constant state of activity with a view to annihilating the English settlements of North America, and the only safety the colonies had was in overawing their enemies and making them feel the weight of their enmity on every possible occasion. This they were enabled to do through the privateers fitted from Charles Town, and the constant presence of these fearless free-lances on the coast preserved Carolina from frequent and disastrous invasion from the South.

In those rude days the line between privateering and pirating was not very strongly marked, and when a few years after the settlement of Carolina, peace was made with Spain by England, these bold rovers, who had done so much for the Crown in time of war, had no idea of permitting their occupation to be taken from them by so small a thing as a

---

[1] Hewat in Carroll, Vol. I., p. 172. The copper elephant coin, struck in 1694, bearing the legend " God save Carolina and the Lords Proprietors," was probably only a medal, and was not known to be in actual circulation though said to be a half-penny. No inscription on it indicated any special value. This condition noted as existing in Carolina also obtained in New England at an earlier period. See Weeden's Economic and Social Hist. of New England, p. 151.

treaty patched up between the contending powers. The sea was wide, and if they should plunder a ship or two in the course of a voyage, and maroon the crews on a desert island, who would be any the wiser? The English authorities evidently were little concerned about their depredations, as their commissions were not even revoked until 1672, and the Carolinians with whom they spent much of their now ill-got gold did not consider it any of their business how their, adventurous friends employed themselves on their long, mysterious cruises. They paid their scores like honest fellows, and paid them in broad gold pieces at that; they interfered with no man, and conducted themselves in as respectable a manner as any sailor on shore-leave was expected to do; and so neither peace officer nor public deemed it their duty to inquire too closely into the conduct of their visitors while they were on the high seas. True, their vessels were never fitted as the colonists were accustomed to seeing merchantmen fitted; but that, again, was the business of nobody but the skipper and his crew, and if he chose to go to sea constantly without a cargo, and seldom troubled himself about securing passports or clearance papers, that was his own concern, and the king had no officer in Carolina at that time who thought it his duty to inquire into these evident irregularities.[1]

There was nothing that contributed so much to the fostering of piracy in the western world as the operations of the English Navigation laws. Did time permit, it would be most interesting to pause and review in detail the history of these famous acts, but we must confine ourselves to the effect they had on the commerce of America, and to how they were instrumental in vitiating the entire business system of the colonies. The first glimpses we have of them are found in 1381 and 1390, during the reign of Richard II. In 1485, under Henry VII., we again find the policy showing itself in legislation, but its growth was slow, and it was not

---

[1] Charles Town had no customs officer until 1685.

until 1651 that it was fully matured and set forth in an act of the Long Parliament, under the direction of Cromwell.[1] The confusion which followed upon the death of the Protector, some years later, enabled the colonists to ignore them with comparative impunity, but upon the Restoration, Charles II. had them re-enacted and enforced with much severity.[2] A further enactment in 1663 imposed still more rigorous restrictions,[3] and in 1672 intercolonial trade was also checked by heavy tariffs.[4]

These Navigation Acts have from time to time been the subject of commendation by numerous English economic and historical writers, especially those of the protection school of the first half of the present century. They have been boastingly styled the " Charta Maritima," the " palladium "[5] of England and of English commerce. Even Adam Smith, while denying their economic efficacy, considering the relations then existing between England and Holland, justified them on the plea of the necessity for national defense,[6] and Sir Archibald Alison, fortifying himself behind a dishonest quotation from Smith, has celebrated in glowing periods " the pitch of grandeur unknown in any other age or country " to which their operations raised England.[7] But strange as it may seem, none of these writers, though dealing with a question of colonial policy, in their survey of the subject looked beyond the southern half of the island of Great Britain. In this they only followed the example of the framers of the acts, and no thought was given to their possible effect in retarding the commercial growth and prosperity of those vast undeveloped lands which were destined in time to outstrip the mother-country and become the

---

[1] See Waterston's Cyclopaedia of Commerce (1863), p. 488.
[2] 13 Car. II., Ch. 14.   [3] 15 Car. II., Ch. 17.
[4] 25 Car. II., Ch. 6. See Doyle, English in America, Va., Carolinas, etc., p. 233.
[5] Quarterly Review, Vol. 28 (1823), p. 431.
[6] Wealth of Nations, Book IV., Chap. II.
[7] Essays, Vol. I., p. 476.

" Greater Britain " of later centuries. If they were the " Charta Maritima " of England, they were indeed the " Charta Pirata " of England's American colonies.[1]

To repeat our proposition, these laws acted as the most potent force in causing the toleration of the pirates in America. When the colonists found that they could neither buy nor sell save in an English market, at prices arbitrarily fixed by English merchants, they were quite willing to tolerate the lawless traders who could afford to sell the products of the world's markets at the lowest prices, since they cost them nothing more than a few hard blows which they enjoyed rather than considered a hardship. It paid the colonists to incur the risk of losing their outward-bound cargoes, which were never during this period of any very great value, when by this toleration they were enabled to buy in the cheapest market the world had ever known.

But the friendship of the Carolinians with the pirates is scarcely to be wondered at when we remember that in this they had no less distinguished an exemplar than King Charles himself. Some years previous he had knighted Henry Morgan and commissioned him Governor of Jamaica in recognition of certain exploits at Panama which were of a purely piratical nature, and his general connivance at their crimes was what had given the pirates their strength in the West Indies.[2]

This state of affairs continued for some time, until, growing bolder, the pirates began to extend their operations. They no longer confined their depredations to the commerce of his Catholic Majesty, but if they chanced to meet an English vessel they did not hesitate to order her to heave to and strike her colors, and many a time was the ensign of St. George lowered before the Black Flag.

---

[1] See Winsor, III., 150 for effect of the Acts on Virginia. Berkeley went to England from Virginia in order to protest against them.

[2] Rivers' Early Hist. of S. C., p. 146. Also Hewat in Carroll, Vol. I., p. 86.

Almost immediately after the landing of Sayle the seat of his colony was removed from Port Royal harbor to the original site of Charles Town at Albemarle Point, on the west bank of the Ashley river, a short distance above the site of the present city of Charleston. It proving inconvenient for shipping, however, the people repaired to Oyster Point under Governor West, where the present city was founded in 1680.[1] Shortly after the first settlement, the Cape Fear colony was abandoned, and Charles Town became the chief seat of government for the entire province. It grew in commercial importance, and the toleration of the pirates became a serious annoyance to the English ship-owners who controlled most of the trade. Masters came into London with grievous tales of outrages suffered at the hands of pirates fitted out from Carolina, and it was not long before complaints were heard in the counting-houses of the provincial capital itself. This was, of course, more serious, but ship-owners in Carolina were few, and the pirates still continued to spend their money with a lavish hand, so the colonists took little notice of these murmurings, although of late they had become alarmingly frequent.

By the beginning of the year 1684, however, the complaints began to assume some definite shape and to be heard from persons whose position and influence commanded attention. Sir Thomas Lynch, Governor of Jamaica, filed an information with the Lords of the Committee for Trade and Plantations regarding the depredations of the pirates, and in February of this year the attention of the government was directed to " the great damage that does arise in his Majesty's service by harboring and encouraging pirates in Carolina."[2] As soon as the subject was considered by the English authorities, the Jamaica law against piracy was, by order of the king, sent to Carolina, with instructions that it

---

[1] The site of the Ashley River settlement is still pointed out some miles from Charleston. See note in Carroll, Vol. I., p. 49.

[2] N. C. Col. Rec., Vol. I., p. 347.

be promulgated as a statute of the province.[1]   The government also complained to the Lords Proprietors, which called forth a reply from Lord Craven, the Palatine, in which he resented the charges made by Lynch in quite a spirited tone. He knew, he said, of no flagrant cases, such as had been charged.   One pirate had come into Carolina some time before, but had been convicted, with two of his crew, and hanged in chains at the entrance of the port, " and there hang to this day for an example to others."   He had had the Jamaica law promulgated, however, and hoped that there would be no further cause for complaint.[2]

Although the Proprietors had this act promulgated, it is very questionable if the king had the right to issue such an order.   Under the charter, issued by his own hand, the Proprietors were given the right to make laws for the Province " by and with the advice, assent, and approbation of the freemen of the said province,"[3] provided only " that the said laws be consonant to reason, and as near as may be conveniently agreeable to the laws and customs of this our realm of England ";[4] and as long as this condition was complied with, any dictation from England might have been resented with much justice.   Some thirty years later the colonists objected strenuously, and to much effect, to the annulment of some of their acts by the Lords Proprietors,[5] who were their immediate rulers, and they could with much more color of justice have resented the interference of the

---

[1] N. C. Col. Rec., Vol. I., p. 347-48. See also S. C. Hist. Soc. Coll., Vol. I., p. 91. The same order was sent to all the other English colonies in North America at the same time See N. C. Col. Rec., as above. Lynch's complaint did not apply to Carolina alone, although it was the only colony he mentioned by name.

[2] N. C. Col. Rec., Vol. I., p. 348.

[3] See the second charter, 1 S. C. Stats., p. 33.

[4] *Ibid.*, p. 34.

[5] For an exposition of the rights of the people against the Proprietors, see Doyle, Vol. I., p. 330.

king.   Under the proper construction of the charter,[1] which
construction Charles virtually acknowledged in making his
order, no statute, English or otherwise, was of force in
Carolina until passed by the Assembly, and it is clear that
the right to make their own laws would have been practically
abrogated had the colonists been compelled to receive them
ready-made from the Crown.   And had they refused to obey
the order the king could have had no redress save by *quo
warranto* proceedings to test the question of the violation of
the charter, or by a writ of *scire facias* to recall it.[2]   The
method of enacting laws in the early days of the colony is
given by a contemporary writer[3] as follows: "The General
Assembly first peruse all English Acts of Parliament, draw
up an account of as many intire ones, and parts of others as
are fit for this Province, and by an Act of Assembly mentioning these Acts, they put them in force."   According to
the same authority the common law of England was not in
force in Carolina until so declared by statute.   It is certain
that the Great Charter of 9 Henry III. was not binding in
the Province until so declared in 1712.[4]

No question was raised, however, as to the legality of the
king's action, and the law, which was destined to become a
dead-letter immediately, was published in the Province.
While there is no way of ascertaining positively, it is reason-
ably certain that the statute against privateers and pirates,
enacted at the legislative session of November, 1685, was in

---

[1] "The charter reserved to the King only allegiance and sov-
ereignty; in all other respects the Proprietors were absolute lords,
with no other service or duty to their monarch than the annual
payment of a trifling sum of money; or in case gold or silver should
be found, a fourth part thereof." W. J. Rivers in Winsor's Narrative and Critical History of America, Vol. V., Art. "The Carolinas,"
p. 290.

[2] See Dalcho's Church History, p. 69, for case of the Church acts.
Also Bancroft I., p. 402 *et seq.*, for similar proceedings in the Mass.
case.

[3] A Letter from S. C. written by a Swiss gentleman in 1710, p.
24 (London ed. 1732).

[4] 2 S. C. Stats., p. 403.

pursuance of this order of King Charles.¹   This act is interesting on account of the naïve manner in which the Solons
of the time disclaimed the guilt of the province and sought
to shift it to other shoulders.   " Whereas," they said, "not
only against such treaties of peace made by his Majestie with
his Allies, but alsoe contrary to his Majestie's Royal Proclamation, severall of his subjects have, and do continually
goe from other English Colonies, and may hereafter from
this Colony, into the service of foreign princes, and saile
under their commissions, contrary to their duty and good
allegiance, and by faire means cannot be restrained from soe
doing, be it therefore enacted," etc.   Not only does this act
refer to privateers, however, but, in more direct obedience to
the royal mandate, clauses were inserted looking to the immediate suppression of the kindred and more heinous crime
of piracy.   We have no records of any court proceedings
against offenders prior to this time, but section IV. of this
act would seem to indicate that there had been such, as all
such prior proceedings were now " ratified, confirmed and
adjudged lawful."

Having obeyed the letter of his Majesty's commands like
faithful subjects, and thus averting further suspicion, the
Carolinians were in a better position to encourage and assist
their buccaneering patrons than before.   Few convictions,
if any, were obtained, and the pirates plied their nefarious
trade with equal security as formerly.   During the war
between France and Spain in 1684 privateers were sent out
from Carolina in a most public manner, and it was an open
secret that their commissions, illegal as they were, were but
cloaks for the most disgraceful piracies.   Learning of these
circumstances, Charles ordered that no more commissions

---

¹ 2 S. C. Stats., p. 7.   This act was passed after Charles' death,
but that circumstance does not make it less probable that it was
in accordance with his orders.   A full description of the Jamaica
Act is given in N. J. Archives, 1st Series, Vol. II., p. 281 *et seq.*,
and its terms correspond generally to the terms of this statute.
² Rivers, p. 146.

should be issued. His commands were but little regarded, however, and the following year, when James II. mounted the throne, he found the commerce of the New World suffering greatly from the pirates, who had by this time established thriving headquarters in the West Indies and the more unsettled parts of the Carolina coast.

One of the few redeeming features of James' brief and turbulent reign was his conduct of naval affairs, and this difficulty which confronted him on his accession he prided himself he could speedily overcome. One of his earliest acts was to venture on the same doubtful ground occupied by Charles, and order a law for the suppression of piracy to be enacted by the Carolina Assembly. The people again proved their loyalty, and the act was entered among the statutes of the Province. It was probably in pursuance of this order that the act " For the Suppressing and Punishing Privateers and Pirattes," etc., was passed by the Assembly in February, 1687.[1] This statute was in large part a re-enactment of that of November, 1685, although its terms applied much more particularly to actual pirates, and provided somewhat more explicitly for the punishment of those who might tolerate or connive at, infractions of the law.

But James had a severer task before him than he had anticipated. The simple passage of an act by a subservient Assembly was not sufficient to wipe out an evil which had been growing for years, and one that was probably very profitable to those into whose hands the duty of extirpating it was reposed. Although the buccaneers no longer sacked the cities of the Spanish Main, or held high carnival in the security of their Jamaican retreat, their strength had by no means been broken, and they were yet so powerful as to be able to make terms—tacit though they were—with the highest officials of the provincial government. In April, 1684, Sir Richard Kyrle, an Irish nobleman, was commis-

---

[1] 2 S. C. Stat., p. 25.

sioned Governor of Carolina.[1] He died very soon after reaching the Province, and Robert Quarry, the Secretary, assumed control of the government without authority from the Proprietors.[2] Quarry was a man of considerable distinction, and had held numerous offices of trust in the colony. A few months before, it had been recommended that "as the governor will not in all probability always reside in Charles Town, which is so near the sea as to be in danger from a sudden invasion of pirates," Governor Kyrle should "commissionate a particular governor for Charles Town who may act in his absence," and Quarry was suggested as a suitable person for this office.[3] It was probably this recommendation that made Quarry feel justified in assuming control when Kyrle died, but when he found himself at the head of affairs his cupidity proved stronger than his honesty. So flagrant was his encouragement of pirates that within two months he was removed from office, and also deprived of his regular position as Secretary.[4] It is evident, however, that the tribunal of public opinion did not adjudge him guilty of any great moral crime, as he remained in the Province and was for years afterwards continued in positions of responsibility.[5]

---

[1] S. C. Hist. Soc. Coll., Vol. I., p. 111.

[2] Props. to Sothell, Rivers, p. 417.

[3] S. C. Hist. Soc. Coll., Vol. I., p. 111.

[4] Props. to Sothell, Rivers, p. 147.

[5] Quarry was one of the most remarkable men in the American colonies during this period, and despite the disgrace which attached to him in consequence of this affair, seems to have maintained a high position until his death. His name appears signed as one of the Council to the South Carolina Acts as late as Nov. 23rd, 1685, and he was Sheriff of Berkeley County just before Ludwell's accession in 1691 (see N. C. Col. Rec., Vol. I., p. 382). Despite the continued opposition of the Proprietors, we find him Vice-Admiral of Carolina in 1701 (see S. C. Hist. Soc. Coll., Vol. II., p. 205). A few years later he went north and succeeded Edward Randolph as Surveyor-General of his Majesty's customs in America. Later he was appointed Admiralty Judge for New York and Pennsylvania, and was member of the Councils of five of the Northern

The attitude of the Carolinians toward the pirates not only reflected infamy on the Province—which, however, they did not seem to feel very keenly—but it was not long before they began to reap the fruit of their disgraceful connections. There had always been a very bitter feeling existing between the colony at Charles Town and the Spaniards at St. Augustine. It was an article of the seventeenth-century Englishman's religious faith to hate a Spaniard as he would the Evil One himself; and the Spaniards not only returned the detestation with interest, but in the present case it was aggravated by the fact that, despite the terms of the treaty of Madrid of 1670, which secured to England all her American possessions against any previous claims Spain may have had,[1] they considered the colonists at Charles Town as intruders on their territory, and chafed continually under their inability to exterminate them as they had done the French settlers of the previous century. The pirates, too, were the open enemies of the Spaniards, and it was but natural that they should have viewed with a redoubled hatred a people who encouraged and fostered the outlaws who had for so many decades made the sea absolutely unsafe for their commerce. Their resentment had been smouldering for a long time, and finally towards the end of the year 1686 it broke out in open hostilities. Three galleys from St. Augustine landed at Edisto, several leagues below Charles Town, and laid waste the plantations in the vicinity, including

---

colonies at one time. His reports to the English government, which were many and voluminous, indicate that he was a special agent of the crown to report from time to time on the condition of the colonies (see N. J. Archives, 1st Series, Vol. II., p. 280). Despite the reproach of his early life, he seems to have performed his duty well, winning the high esteem of both the colonists and the home authorities. This makes it seem possible that his career in Carolina was not so dark as the documents of the time indicate. He died about 1712-13 (see N. J. Archives, 1st Series, Vol. IV., p. 175).

[1] Rivers, p. 82. The Spaniards knew Charles Town harbor as St. George's Bay.

those of Governor Morton and Secretary Paul Grimball, and killed the former's brother-in-law. They then pushed on to Port Royal, and completely destroyed the Scotch colony there, and retired before a force could be raised to oppose them.[1] The colonists were overwhelmed with anger and indignation at the barbarity of this sudden invasion, and began immediate preparations to avenge it by a descent upon St. Augustine. An expedition was organized and an armament about to sail, when James Colleton, who had been commissioned Governor the previous August, arrived from the Barbadoes. He immediately assumed the reins of government, and ordered the expedition to disband. Some of the leaders demurred, whereupon he threatened to hang every man who would not instantly come on shore and abandon his purpose. These peremptory measures, although humiliating to the settlers, nipped in the bud a war which would have been long and bloody and for which the colony was by no means prepared. The Carolinians considered the abandonment of the enterprise as a stain upon English honor, but they were given little satisfaction from the Proprietors. Their complaints only elicited the reply that they could expect nothing but that the Spaniards would retaliate on them for harboring and assisting the lawless rovers who maintained themselves by preying on the commerce of the Spanish settlements.[2]

Colleton commenced his administration during a turbulent era. For a long time the pirates had been permitted free access to Charles Town, and Joseph Morton, who had succeeded Quarry, had even given formal permission to two buccaneers to bring some Spanish prizes into the

---

[1] By some strange error, Doyle has antedated this invasion by six years (see p. 358). This error is remarkable, considering how much he relies on Rivers. Mr. Thwaites in his recent work on the colonies in the Epochs of Am. History series makes the same mistake.

[2] Carolina Entry Book, Vol. I., p. 106, quoted in Chalmers, Polit. Annals, p. 547; also Rivers, p. 145.

harbor, and had also, with the sanction of the Council, allowed the infamous Morgan to come into the province.[1]

One of the first acts of Colleton's administration was the expulsion of John Boon from the Council "for holding correspondence with pirates."[2] He had special instructions regarding the suppression of piracy, and in every way he did his best to stamp out the evil, but only with partial success. Finally the situation became so serious that the home government was compelled to take some decisive action. Accordingly in 1687 King James commissioned Sir Robert Holmes to proceed to the West Indies with a fleet and to make short work of all the pirates in those and adjacent waters. At the same time orders went from Whitehall to Carolina to seize all pirates who came into the province and hold them at the pleasure of the king, and certain unwarrantable practices, which had been used to facilitate their acquittal, were ordered to be suppressed.[3] A copy of the commission issued to Holmes was also transmitted by Lords Craven and Carteret, two of the Proprietors, with instructions to assist in every way in extirpating the outlaws.[4]

Just what assistance the Carolinians gave Holmes is not known, but it is not probable that they troubled themselves to detain many prisoners at his Majesty's pleasure. They complied with the instructions, however, and enacted a law not only against all pirates, but against all suspects, and provided for the issuance of commissions for the trial of offenders.[5] Holmes was far from making a permanent success of his undertaking, but his presence on the North American coast, and the apparent determination of the king

---

[1] Rivers, p. 147.

[2] See instructions from Props., S. C. Hist. Soc. Coll., Vol. I., p. 118.

[3] S. C. Hist. Soc. Coll., Vol. I., p. 120.

[4] N. C. Rec., Vol. I., 354. Rivers, p. 147.

[5] 2 S. C. Stats., p. 25.

and the Proprietors, had the effect of stopping for a time the indulgence which had been so freely granted to the freebooters.

The most casual observer of Carolina history can perceive that long before the period at which we have now arrived, the colonists had conceived very much of a contempt for the authority of the Lords Proprietors. They were loyal enough to the British government, but they held but slack allegiance to their immediate rulers. From them they received scant consideration, and it is not surprising that their loyalty should not have been of a very ardent nature. Nor did they lack justification for this sentiment. Their grievances against the Proprietors were not a few. The fact that they were compelled to pay their quit-rents in money, instead of in produce, was a source of constant irritation, and not infrequently of real distress. The action of the Proprietors in regard to the expedition against St. Augustine also engendered much bitterness, and no little jealousy was caused by the special favor shown to the Scotch followers of Lord Cardross at Port Royal, and to the newly-arrived French Huguenots.[1] Consequently the colonists yielded little obedience to the Proprietors' instructions, except when forced to it by such peremptory measures as were adopted by Colleton to stop the late armament against the Spaniards; and they could hardly have been expected to resign so profitable a connection as that with the pirates, merely at the command of a board of gentlemen three thousand miles across the sea, who only looked upon the colony as an enterprise for the betterment of their private fortunes.

But Colleton did his utmost in the face of every difficulty to enforce a proper observance of the laws, and whatever other lawlessness may have prevailed during his administration, the pirates were received in Charles Town with less favor than in many years. But however strenuously he

---

[1] Doyle, p. 362.

attempted to do his duty, he was seriously handicapped by the action of the Proprietors, which had for some time been most arbitrary. It was about this period that a contest arose between the Governor and the Proprietors on one side, and the Colonial Assembly on the other, which was, of course in a very modified degree, somewhat of a parallel to the great contest between the King and the Commons, which a half-century previous had culminated in the great rebellion in England.

The struggle had been in progress for some time when in 1689 the Proprietors ordered Colleton and their deputies[1] to convene no more Assemblies, without specific instructions, except in cases of extraordinary necessity.[2] As the laws were enacted for a term of only twenty-three months,[3] in 1690 the Province found itself without a single statute in force.[4] This was indeed an unfortunate state of affairs. It had been with the greatest difficulty that the laws against piracy had been enforced at all, and now that they had expired by limitation it was only to be expected that within a few months the entire coast would be overrun by them. Governor Colleton did not deem this one of the " extraordinary occasions " which the Proprietors had excepted in their instructions, and instead of calling an Assembly in order to meet the exigency, he declared the Province to be under military rule.[5] It would hardly be fair to criticise him for this action, however, because, had he convened an Assembly, it is probable that nothing would have been done. The point of dispute was the claim of the popular House

---

[1] The Proprietors' deputies with the Governor and a number of members elected by the Commons House, constituted the " Upper House " of the Assembly. See Winsor, Vol. V., p. 307, for the method of choosing them at the time of the founding of the colony.

[2] Props. to Sothell, May 12th, 1691: Rivers, 432.

[3] Fundamental Constitutions LXXVI. Many statutes contained a provision for their expiration at the end of this period.

[4] Address to Sothell. Rivers, p. 423.

[5] *Ibid.*

that a bill did not have to "necessarily pass the Grand Council before it be read in Parliament,"[1] and it was not to be supposed that either party would recede from its position. It was claimed that the declaration of martial law was brought about by petitions which had been most irregularly drawn, many signatures having been forged, and great excitement followed upon the proclamation. "Many prepared to leave the cuntrey," says a contemporary account; "but most people were soe weary of the discontents that attended their thoughts upon this illegal, tirannical and oppressive way of Government, that they were more concerned to be provided against their friends and fellow Subjects here, than the publick Enemy abroad, and the ferment grew soe high that nothinge but desperation was generally observed among the people."[2]

Just at this juncture Seth Sothell, one of the Proprietors, arrived in the Province and assumed direction of the government. Colleton was banished, and required to give bail in the sum of £10,000 for his appearance at Westminster to answer to such charges as might be preferred against him.[3] At the same time Stephen Bull and Paul Grimball, members of the Council, and Charles Colleton and Thomas Smith, Sr., were disabled from holding office because of the part they played in encouraging martial rule.[4] Having thus rid himself of his opponents, Sothell commenced an administration which was most remarkable for official outrage, if not deliberate crime.[5] In the meantime the pirates, encouraged by the unsettled condition of the colony, had renewed their relations with their friends in various parts of the Province; and Sothell, under a pretense of enforcing the laws

---

[1] Address to Sothell. Rivers, p. 423.

[2] *Ibid.*

[3] 2 S. C. Stats., pp. 45, 46.

[4] *Ibid.*, p. 49. These acts were annulled by the Proprietors and Grimball was ordered restored to all his honors. See N. C. Col. Rec., Vol. I., p. 382.

[5] See S. C. Hist. Soc. Coll., Vol. I., pp. 126, 127, 128.

against them, took occasion to imprison persons objectionable to him, falsely alleging them to be connected with the piratical trade.[1] The indignation which this aroused doubtless had much to do with causing a reaction in favor of the pirates, and when Philip Ludwell, Sothell's successor,[2] arrived, they were again ingratiating themselves with the people, and promised to give much trouble in the near future.

The new Governor's instructions contained special reference to these outlaws. Wrote the Proprietors: " You are to use your utmost endeavour to seize any Pyrats that shall come to Carolina, and you are to prosecute all such as shall presume to trade with them, or have any commerce with them contrary to law, to all the utmost rigor the law allows."[3] How he succeeded in fulfilling his instructions will be seen. For the better governance of the colony he was also ordered to make an ·effort to consolidate the Assemblies of North and South Carolina at Charles Town.[4]

Ludwell entered upon his office at the beginning of a stormy period. The recent agitations had stirred the colony almost to a point of civil war, and its safety was threatened by foes without and within. The pirates were rising to the height of their power, and were beginning to have very broad notions of the dignity of their position in the world. Their trade at this time had splendid traditions, and the lawless rovers of the sea, proud of the records of their predecessors, were becoming as bold and arrogant as the Barbary monarchs of the African coast. It was with pride that they recalled the time when their power enabled them to turn from the chase of merchant vessels on the high seas to the bombardment of fortified ports, and the sack of the rich and

---

[1] Proprietors to Sothell, May 12, 1691, in Rivers, p. 431. A number of these complaints refer also to the period just preceding this, when Sothell was Governor in N. C.

[2] Commissioned Governor, Nov. 8th, 1691.

[3] N. C. Col. Rec., Vol. I., p. 380.

[4] *Ibid.*

populous cities of the Spanish Main. They remembered with a glow of insolent satisfaction the stern terms to which they had forced the governors of more than one powerful colony, and their more recent successes had filled them with an arrogance which now threatened every port on the Atlantic seaboard with invasion. They no longer sought the toleration of any people with whom they were inclined to trade. What they wished they demanded, and it was not often that any one had the temerity to oppose them with open force.

It has never been clearly shown what encouragement the pirates received at the hands of Governor Sothell during his brief and tyrannical rule, but the rumors of the time were sufficient to justify the Proprietors in ordering Ludwell to examine into charges which had been preferred of granting commissions to pirates, for which he is said to have received substantial reward.[1] The investigation, if it ever took place, amounted to practically nothing, as might have been expected. Sothell was too wise not to cover his tracks behind him, and it is probable that there was no one in the Province who could have ventured to give evidence against him without very seriously implicating himself.

But Ludwell soon found that it was a greater task than he could accomplish to look after the pirates of his own time, much less to successfully investigate their doings during the reign of his predecessor. While no specific blame ever has been attached to him for improperly administering the laws against the freebooters, nor have any such charges ever been made against him, the condition of the Province permitted them to enjoy a greater freedom during his administration than they had done for many years previous. Soon after his accession a crew of forty men arrived in a vessel called the Royal Jamaica, bringing with them large quantities of silver and gold. By means of their wealth they found immediate favor with many of the people, and the officials were

---

[1] N. C. Col. Rec., Vol. I., p. 383.

so far swayed by considerations of which history does not speak, that they were permitted to remain in the Province unmolested, on the condition of their entering into bond to keep the peace for a year, the Proprietors in the meantime being applied to for a grant of indemnity in their favor.[1] Another instance recorded of this administration, showing how the law was disregarded, was the case of a vessel which was wrecked on the coast, the crew of which escaped and came to Charles Town. These men boasted openly of having been on a piratical cruise in the Red Sea, where they had plundered numerous vessels belonging to the Grand Mogul. It is not recorded that any of the villains were ever brought to justice, nor is there any reason to believe that they were even placed under arrest, or required to give bond, as was done in the case of the crew of the Royal Jamaica.[2] Edward Randolph, surveyor-general of his Majesty's customs in America, in reporting the case to the home government, says: " They were entertained, and had liberty to stay or goe to any other place."[3]

Under Ludwell's administration matters grew from bad to worse, until they reached a disgraceful point. The pirates who were brought to trial escaped by shameless bribery of the juries, and some of the highest officials of the courts were not free from imputations of the most corrupt conduct. The Assembly went so far as to pass an act " To provide for Indifferent Jurymen in all causes Civill and Criminall," which the Proprietors annulled on the ground that it was " very unreasonable, and many ways dangerous and tending to the lending [leaving] the most enormous Crimes unpunisht, especially Pyracy."[4] " It will thereby be in the power of the Sheriff," wrote the Proprietors to the

---

[1] Hewat in Carroll's Coll., Vol. I., p. 106.

[2] *Ibid.*

[3] S. C. Hist Soc. Coll., Vol. II., p. 196. Also N. C. Rec., Vol. I., p. 467.

[4] S. C. Commons House Journals, No. 1, p. 58, Props. to Gov. and Deputies, 10th Apr., 1693.

Governor and their deputies, " so to divide the twelve for each paper that there shall be in every paper some notorious favorers of Pyrates who, coming prepared for it, may be able to constraine the rest of the jury to consent to what verdict they please."[1] It is highly probable that the constraint referred to here was that of flagrant bribery in the jury-room. At the same time the Proprietors found it necessary to annul a law which had been enacted governing the election of members of the Assembly. This act was so very loose in its construction that " all the Pyrates that were in the Shipp that had been plundering in the Red Sea had been qualified to vote for Representatives."[2] The only requirement was that the voter should possess ten pounds, or property valued at that amount, and the pirates with their stolen gold were thus qualified as fully as the oldest freeholder in the colony.

But all these measures failed to have the desired effect. Charles Town was completely overrun by pirates who flocked into Carolina from every quarter. By means of their ill-got gold they corrupted the people, and set the law at utter defiance. " The courts of law," says Hewat, " became scenes of altercation, discord and confusion. Bold and seditious speeches were made from the bar in contempt of the Proprietors and their government."[3]

There was, however, a very considerable element in the colony that strove to maintain the honor of the Province, and to have the criminals brought to justice, and in order to counteract its influence, the friends of the pirates determined to take steps to secure their certain immunity. The Governor had no right to grant any pardons except such as were authorized by the Proprietors, and a bill was introduced into the Assembly which convened in September, 1692, which granted complete indemnity to all pirates and their

---

[1] S. C. Commons House Journals, No. 1, p. 58, Props. to Gov. and Deputies, 10th Apr., 1693.
[2] *Ibid.* [3] Hewat in Carroll, Vol. I., pp. 106-107.

accomplices. This was the subject of high and fierce debate, which was, however, interrupted by the receipt of the intelligence from the Governor that he would place his veto upon any such act. Foiled in this, they enacted a law giving the colonial magistrates the power to enforce the English Habeas Corpus Act,[1] and by this means many pirates escaped justice and took up their residence in the colony.[2]

It now seemed practically impossible to do anything to stamp out the evil which had so grafted itself upon the life of the Province. The authority of the Proprietors was powerless when matched against pirate gold, and finally despairing of ever securing justice in the Provincial courts, and desiring to do something to satisfy the colonists, and recover them from their seditious condition, they issued in April, 1693, letters patent, granting full pardon for all offenses committed in Carolina prior to Ludwell's accession, with the exception of piracy, treason and murder.[3] The friends of the pirates were not pacified, however, and the records fail to show that a single one of the freebooters was brought to trial.

This effort to conciliate the colonists seems to have borne some fruit, however. During Ludwell's administration the Province had reached its lowest ebb, both morally and commercially. The lawless element had done its worst and could go no further, and it was time for the tide to turn in the opposite direction. Under the firm and patient administration of one of the Proprietors the reaction came, and we shall soon see how the colony shook off the domination of its most depraved class, and rose to a position of dignity and honor from which it never again receded.

---

[1] 2 S. C. Stats., p. 74. The original of this statute is lost.

[2] Hewat in Carroll, Vol. I., p. 107.

[3] S. C. Hist. Soc. Coll., Vol. I., p. 130. Hewat says the pardon was extended to all pirates except those who had plundered the Grand Mogul's possessions, but I am able to find no verification of this statement.

CHAPTER II.

Governor Ludwell's administration, despite his earnest efforts, had not been a success, and after having held office for a little more than two years, he was superseded by Thomas Smith in November, 1693. Smith was at this time probably the most prominent man in the colony. He had served in Ludwell's Council, and in return for his public services had been elevated by the Proprietors to the provincial nobility, bearing the honorable title of Landgrave. During a period when political virtue was at a discount, he had maintained his integrity unspotted, and by his unswerving adherence to the right, commanded the respect of both friends and enemies. As the leader of the better class of the colonists, it was thought that he would in a short time be able to place Carolina on a peaceful and prosperous footing. Along with his commission,[1] he received instructions to enforce the law against the pirates most rigidly, so that there might no longer be any reason for the charge that these outlaws found a safe retreat in the colony;[2] and to report why the Red Sea pirates, lately come into the Province, had not been brought to trial.[3] He was also ordered to carry out what Ludwell had failed in, namely, to consolidate the Assemblies of the northern and southern divisions of the Province at Charles Town.[4] But Smith's brief reign was a disappointment to both Proprietors and people. He had been in office less than a year when, despairing of peace

---

[1] A facsimile of Smith's commission appeared in Harper's Magazine for December, 1875.

[2] Instructions to Smith, S. C. Hist. Soc. Coll., Vol. I., p. 135.

[3] S. C. Hist. Soc. Coll., Vol. I., p. 134.

[4] *Ibid.*

and order, he wrote to the Proprietors resigning his post, and announcing that he and a number of other gentlemen had determined to leave Carolina and seek homes in a less turbulent part of America.[1]   " It was impossible," he said, " to settle the country unless a Proprietor himself was sent over with full power to heal their grievances,"[2] and without waiting to hear from England, he vacated the office, leaving Joseph Blake in charge of affairs.

As might have been expected, the pirates were only friendly to the Carolinians as long as it was to their interest to be so.   The Proprietors had not yet been able to do anything for the colony when the people were thrown into a state of consternation by reports that the outlaws were preparing " to attempt the plundering and burning " of Charles Town.   Memories of the sack of Panama and Porto Bello, and of the appalling atrocities which followed upon the fall of Maracaibo, a quarter of a century before, were recalled by the old settlers, and the terrified people in anticipation saw their city go up in smoke and flame, and beheld its embers quenched in the blood of defenseless women and children. The Assembly met, and a petition was hurried across the ocean, in which the circumstances were narrated, and particular emphasis laid on the urgent necessity of fortifying the harbor.[3]   But weeks passed without any hostile demonstrations on the part of the pirates, the panic which the threats and rumors had produced subsided, and in a short time the terrors of the people were forgotten.

The Proprietors, who received the desperate news in a most philosophical manner, and seemed to care little for the fate of the colony, had in the meantime acted upon Governor Smith's resignation, and followed his suggestion in regard

---

[1] S. C. Hist. Soc. Coll., Vol. I., p. 135.   Smith did not leave the colony, but died shortly after this.   See *Ibid.*, p. 138.

[2] Archdale in Carroll, Vol. II., p. 101.

[3] S. C. Commons House Journals, No. 1, p. 104.   This petition was dated Feb. 5th, 1695.

to sending one of their number to Carolina. They first selected a grandson of the great Earl of Shaftesbury for the mission, but the young nobleman preferred a life of luxury in London to the hardships of a residence in the wilds of America, and promptly declined the appointment. They then chose John Archdale, a Quaker Proprietor, and sent him out, armed with all the powers of a dictator, to bring the Province back to a state of peace.

Whatever Smith's failure on other points may have been, he had succeeded in at least one instance in enforcing the pirate law in a more rigid manner than had been done in many years. He had reported to the Proprietors the full proceedings of the trials and convictions, and when Archdale arrived about the middle of the year 1695, he found instructions awaiting him regarding a number of the freebooters who had been reprieved until the pleasure of the English authorities concerning them could be learned. These instructions were fully consistent with the wavering policy the Proprietors had always followed concerning the punishment of crime in the Province. Although they had directed Smith to enforce the law against the pirates with the utmost severity, and had inquired somewhat sharply into the failure of Governor Ludwell to bring the Red Sea outlaws to justice, now that convictions were secured, they ordered Archdale to pardon the condemned men, and transport them to whatever place he saw fit.[1]

Archdale's mild but firm rule did much to allay the troubles of the colony, and the seeming willingness of the people to forget their political differences indicated that much of their previous trouble had been due to the fact that the governors either could not, or would not, understand them and their needs. But in spite of all his efforts for the good of Carolina, Archdale did not escape the charge of encouraging, and even dealing with, the pirates. Edward Randolph reported that he had harbored the outlaws, and

---

[1] S. C. Hist. Soc. Coll., Vol. I., p. 138.

had been paid for his indulgence toward them.[1] These charges, which were not made until some time after Archdale had retired from the government, also implicated his successor, Joseph Blake, and Vice-Admiralty Judge Morton.[2] Several alleged cases were cited in the report, and Randolph, in commenting on them, recommended as the remedy that the Crown assume control of Carolina and all other proprietaries in America.[3] Fortunately for the good name of the accused officials, Randolph's statements are not to be taken as good evidence in matters concerning the colonies. His notorious unreliability and his bitter prejudice against everything American, has been clearly shown in the history of New England of this period,[4] and the names of the Carolina officials have suffered no taint in consequence of his charges. At the time, however, they had the effect of bringing a letter from the Board of Trade to the Proprietors, complaining that his Majesty had been informed of these irregularities, and warning them that they must not be repeated " under the severest penalties." It is but just to add that when the pirate Every was tried in England, much damaging testimony regarding Carolina was brought out, and it was alleged that the pirate Want was at that time fitted out from the Province. The Proprietors were commanded to apprehend all pirates who might come into Carolina, and to make a report on the subject at an early day.[5]

Randolph's complaints were by no means leveled at Carolina alone, and although he is quite explicit in mentioning

---

[1] " Mr. John Archdale, the late Govr., permitted some of Every's Men who came from Providence to Land, and bring their money quietly a shoar, for which favour he was well paid by them."— Randolph to Lords Commissioners for Trade, N. C. Col. Recs., Vol. I., p. 545.

[2] N. C. Col. Rec., Vol. I., p. 546.

[3] *Ibid.*, p. 548.

[4] See Hutchinson's Mass., Vol. I., pp. 319, 329. Also Chalmers I., pp. 320, 406, 409.

[5] N. C. Col. Rec., Vol. I., p. 475. Also S. C. Hist. Soc. Coll., Vol. I., pp. 204, 205.

that Province, it was a fact that at this time nearly every colony in America was, in one way or another, offering encouragement to the pirates. The minutes of the Provincial Council of Pennsylvania teem with notices of the freebooters on that coast, and were all the references given, the array would weary the eye of the reader; in the first volume alone no less than twenty-one are to be found; in the second, thirteen; and in the third, eight. This is without including a number of minor notices from which no clear inferences can be drawn. Watson is the authority for the statement that about this time a son of Deputy Governor Markham, of this Province, was denied a seat in the House because of his dealings with pirates.[1] In New England the situation was but little better. The same " embarrassment of riches " is encountered in the records here as in Pennsylvania, and the reader is referred to the indices to the Massachusetts Historical Society Papers, to Arnold's History of Rhode Island, and to Mr. Weeden's Economic and Social History of New England, where the notices will be found in sufficient quantity to satisfy the most capacious historical maw. Every one is familiar with the culpability of Governor Fletcher of New York and his secretary, Nicholls. So notorious was Fletcher's connection with the freebooters that his successor, Lord Bellamont, recommended that he be sent to England to be tried for piracy; but for some unknown reason the recommendation was never carried out.[2]

Archdale vacated the Governorship in South Carolina in 1696, appointing Joseph Blake, his nephew, as his successor. Blake's administration was a peaceful one, although it was during his term of office that the renewed complaints came from his Majesty's Council to the Proprietors[3] concerning the Carolina pirates. An examination of these complaints shows quite conclusively that though Blake's name was

---

[1] Annals of Philadelphia, Vol. II., p. 216 *et seq.*

[2] See also N. J. Archives, 1st Series, Vol. II., pp. 157-162.

[3] S. C. Hist. Society Coll., Vol. I., pp. 205, 206, 207.

directly connected with them, they were but repetitions of the
old charges of several years before, and that there were no
new cases upon which they were based. The Proprietors,
however, sent over the Jamaica law against piracy for pro-
mulgation. The contemporaneous records do not give the
previous history of this act, but it was in all probability the
same old law which had been promulgated years before at
the command of Charles II., and which had either become
a dead letter in the Province, or had been permitted to expire by limitation.

This act, with the accompanying instructions from the
Proprietors, was brought into the Assembly on September
19th, 1698, and was made a special order for the 22d of the
same month. On that day the House resolved itself into a
" Grand Committee," with Dr. Charles Burnham in the
chair. It seems that the committee, with commendable independence, determined not to swallow the Jamaica act
whole, but to prepare a new one, retaining all the chief features of the other. Accordingly it was agreed to report the
following resolutions:

" Resolved, That a Bill be Drawn up for the Method of
Trying Privateers and Pirates.

" Resolved, That it shall be fellony for any subject of the
Kingdom of England to serve any prince or potentate
whatsoever in an hostile manner against his said Majesty or
any of his subjects.

" Resolved, That the act doe provide for the tryall of all
treasonous fellonies, pyracies, roberies, murders, or confederacies that shall hereafter be committed upon the seas
where the Admiral hath jurisdiction.

" Resolved, All former proceedings against the aforesaid
offenders be ratified,[1] and all officers indemnified.

" Resolved, That those who hold correspondence with
such persons after proclamation shall be fined or imprisoned.

---

[1] This has general reference to the class of criminals mentioned
in the foregoing sections, and not to any special offenders.

" Resolved, That power be given to commission officers to raise forces for apprehending pyrates after proclamation."

On the committee rising, and the speaker resuming the chair, the House adopted the above report, and ordered " that a Bill for restraining and Punishing Privateers and Pyrates [be] committed to Doctr. Charles Burnham, Mr. John Buchley, and Mr. Robert Hall to be repaired [prepared]." The next day " A bill for the restraining and punishing of privateers and pirates " was read " the first time and passed with amendments."[1] The word " passed " as used here cannot mean that it became a statute on this occasion, as the rule was that all bills should be " read three several times on three several days, in each house,"[2] before they could pass into laws. The journals contain no further reference to it until a session which was held two months later, and it is certain that it was either defeated, or lost in a rush of bills on the calendar. On the 19th of November " the Humble Address and Remonstrance of the Members of the House of Commons " to the Proprietors, complained " that the Government pretends to putt in practice and force an Act entitled an Act for the restraining of Privateers and Pyrates, dated the —— day of —— which was never made according to any of your Lordshipps Instructions, Rules of Government, and Constitutions, nor with the consent of the major part of the delegates of the people, and which also wants a confirmation under hand and seal in open Assembly."[3] Whether this remonstrance arose from a desire to protect the pirates, or from a simple desire to protest against usurpation of authority on the part of the government, is not known, but the occasion of it is very evident. The Governor and the Lords Proprietors' Deputies, constituting the " Upper House " of the Assembly, had sent the bill to the

---

[1] See S. C. Commons House Journals, No. 1, pp. 189, 191, 192, 193, for a history of this measure.

[2] " A Letter from S. C.," p. 23.

[3] S. C. Commons House Journals, No. 1, p. 215.

Commons " for their concurrence."[1]   The Commons had not concurred, and occasion having arisen for the enforcement of some law against the pirates, the government assumed the responsibility of enforcing the terms of the Jamaica act which had failed of passage in the House.   Hence the remonstrance on the part of the latter.

Although the prosperity of the pirates was undoubtedly waning, they still continued such a menace to American commerce that in 1699 the English authorities realized that mild measures would no longer have any effect, and proceeded to pass through Parliament an act of such severity as to drive the greater part of the outlaws from the American seas.[2]   This act was largely a revival of the act of 28 Henry VIII.   It recited the great inconvenience incident to the transportation of pirates from distant colonies to England for trial, and authorized their trial on shipboard or on land by certain officers who were to be constituted commissioners for that purpose.   The court was to consist of seven members, any three of whom could organize it for business. A colonial Governor, or Lieutenant-Governor, a member of Council, or a commander of one of his Majesty's ships, must be on the commission, and all members were called upon to subscribe to a specially prepared oath before they could sit in judgment on any case.   After hearing the testimony in open court, the judges were to hold a private session and determine the guilt or innocence of the accused by a majority vote.   Presumably on a modification of the principle of he who lives by the sword shall perish by the sword, it was provided that the condemned should be put to death " in such place upon the Sea, or within the Ebbing and Flowing thereof as the President, or the major part of the Court " might appoint.   It was also enacted that " whereas severall evill disposed persons in the Plantations and elsewhere have contributed very much toward the Encrease and

---

[1] S. C. Commons House Journals, No. 1, p. 189.

[2] Statutes of the Realm, 11 W. and M.

Encouragement of Pirates by setting them forth, and by aiding, abetting, receiveing and concealeing them and their Goods, and there being some Defects in the Law for bringing such evill disposed Persons to condign Punishment," all such persons after the 29th of September, 1700, should be adjudged pirates and dealt with accordingly. Special pensions were also guaranteed to persons who might be wounded in expeditions against the pirates, and in the event of any volunteers being killed, it was provided that their families should be provided for by the government. Rewards were also offered to informers, and in cases where the colonial officers refused to assist in suppressing piracy, the charter of the colony was to be forfeited to the Crown. Masters of vessels marooning any of their crew, or leaving them in distant parts, thus throwing in their way the temptation " to go upon the grand account "—to use the old phrase—were liable to conviction and imprisonment. This act was to be in force for a period of seven years. By an act of 6 Anne this statute was renewed for a like term of years, and by an act of 1 George I. was again continued for five years.[1] During the year 1708 a general pardon was declared throughout the British dominions, from which pirates were expressly excepted, although this was not necessary, as by the common law they could not be included in the operation of general pardons.

During the last years of Blake's administration several occurrences were recorded which indicate that the South Carolinians were well aroused to a sense of the infamy which attached to them from their connection with the pirates, although it is not improbable that they were brought to this mind largely by the losses which they themselves were now suffering from piratical depredations. The new and purer condition of public sentiment which followed upon the administration of Governor Archdale was, during the last decade of the century, greatly strengthened by a change in

---

[1] N. C. Col. Rec., Vol. II., 319.

the industrial life of the Province, brought about by the introduction of rice. Previous to this time South Carolina had had no staple crop, her exports being of a miscellaneous character, and constantly varying in quantity. In common with all the other English colonies, South Carolina had been greatly affected by the operations of the Navigation Acts, but now, after the lapse of years, the condition changed. Although still forced to sell in a single market, at prices little influenced by demand and supply, the Carolina planters saw that they had opportunities of becoming rich off the proceeds of their great rice plantations.[1] In 1699 the crop was so extensive that, owing to the loss of many Carolina vessels in the war between France and Spain,[2] sufficient tonnage could not be found to transport the crop to the markets on the other side of the water. Rice was a most profitable export, although as a matter of course the profits depended entirely on its safe arrival in England. The Carolinians therefore began to be very much annoyed when their valuable cargoes were captured by the pirates, and they soon learned to look upon their former friends and allies with a distrust which developed into a hatred which made Charles Town no longer a safe or pleasant residence for the depredators.

During this year a party of about forty-five men—English, French, Portuguese, and Indians—attracted by the spoil that awaited them, set out on a piratical cruise from Havanna. They lay in the vicinity of Charles Town for some time, taking several vessels belonging to the Province, which they retained and adapted to their own uses, after

---

[1] One reason of this was that England permitted the colonies to send to other countries such exports as were not wanted at home, and England does not seem to have been a great rice consuming country. I have not the statement of exports for this period, but for the period between 1720 and 1730 only 30,000 bbls. of rice went to England, Ireland and other plantations, against 83,379 to Portugal alone, and 372,118 to Holland, Hamburg, Bremen, Sweden and Denmark. See Courtenay's Year Book for 1880, p. 245.

[2] Edward Randolph in S. C. Hist. Soc. Coll., Vol. I., p. 211.

sending the crews on shore. They had not been on the Carolina coast many weeks, however, before they quarreled over their spoil, and the Europeans and Indians combined against the Englishmen, and turned them adrift at sea. After numerous hardships, the abandoned party landed at Sewee, now Bull's, Bay, and came to Charles Town overland, where they told an ingeniously concocted story of having been shipwrecked on the coast. Unfortunately for them, however, the masters of three vessels they had recently taken, happened to be in Charles Town, and recognized them without difficulty as their captors of a few weeks before. They were immediately apprehended and condemned to death, the sentence being executed on seven out of the nine.[1]

This must have occurred before the news of the English act reached the Province, and followed within a short time, as it probably was, by the intelligence of the severe measures the home authorities were preparing to enforce, it resulted in almost the entire extermination of the pirates in Carolina, and they did not show themselves on the coast again for many years.

Soon after, a number of pirates came into Charles Town with declarations of their intentions to abandon their evil ways; and there being no evidence against them on which they could be convicted, they were permitted to live undisturbed in the Province.

The manuscript records now preserved in the Probate Court of Charleston indicate some peculiar practices that were in vogue in that day. Among them is a power of attorney filed by one Samuel Saltus of Bermuda, delegating to John Jones, locksmith, the right to sue in his behalf for the recovery of a certain sloop which had been captured from him by one Lewis Ferdinando, a pirate, and his company, if she should at any time be brought into Carolina.[2] Accompanying this is an order issued by Governor Blake,

---

[1] Hewat in Carroll, Vol. I., p. 127.
[2] Probate Court MS. Rec., Charleston County, 1694-1704, p. 244.

that Matthew Tyrer should not again be put in jeopardy of his life on the charge of taking this sloop, as he had been accused before the Grand Jury and acquitted.[1]

Having promulgated the act of 1699, King William was not disposed to be too severe on those who might wish to stop their career of crime, and enter once more upon an honest life. Accordingly, in March, 1701, he proclaimed an Act of Grace, offering pardon for all piracies committed prior to June 24th, 1701, provided the outlaws would surrender and take the oath of allegiance within twelve months. Several pirates who had sailed with the notorious Kidd were in the Province, and they promptly surrendered and took the oath. Just how many of Kidd's crew were in Carolina at this time is not known, but there was evidently quite a number of them. In a letter to the Lords of Trade, dated from Philadelphia, February 28th, 1701, William Penn mentions Kidd's men as having settled in Carolina as planters, with one Rayner, their captain.[2] In 1700 Blake died, and was succeeded by James Moore, several of whose pardons to pirates can be seen in the Probate Court records, previously quoted. Numerous interesting affidavits in connection with these pardons have also been preserved.[3]

One of the last notices of the pirates of this period is found in the MS. Journals of the Assembly. In August, 1701, one Peter Painter, having been recommended for the position of public powder-receiver, was rejected by the Upper House. " Mr. Painter," ran the brief message to the Commons, signed by Governor Moore, " Having committed Piracy, and not having his Majesties Pardon for the same, Its resolved he is not fitt for that Trust."[4] There is no record of proceedings ever being instituted against Painter for his alleged crimes, however.

---

[1] Probate Court MS. Rec., Charleston County, 1694-1704, p. 250.
[2] S. C. Hist. Soc. Coll., Vol. I., p. 213.
[3] See above cited records, pp. 297-98.
[4] S. C. Commons House Journal, No. 1, p. 392.

As has been seen, during the last years of the seventeenth century a rapid change came over public opinion regarding piracy and kindred crimes, and whatever their selfish interests may have been, it cannot be charged that the change of view among the colonists was wholly due to these. Carolina was advancing in dignity as a colony. She had begun to attract the attention of the world, and the influential men of Charles Town, the leaders in social and political life, were no longer of the adventurer class which had flocked to these shores thirty years before. Blake, who for a number of years had occupied a prominent position in the colony, had brought with him to America a large following of sturdy, honest, middle-class English Dissenters, who were good types of the latest settlers, and he and his chief adherents were men of integrity, who had come to Carolina with high motives for the extension of the dominion and power of England, and with a worthy pride in the future of this new world. The influx of Huguenots, too, had its effect. These people were now well established in the colony under the special protection of the English government, and although they were still regarded with a jealous eye as aliens and intruders, although they were not encouraged, and in some instances had met with political and even religious persecution, still their numbers and their high moral character had weight. Composing, as they did, the best element of the French masses, and driven from their prosperous homes in the fairest provinces of France because they would not yield their consciences to the corrupt standards of that abandoned age, it was only natural that they should view with abhorrence the toleration of these lawless hordes of sea-robbers. It was true that they had as yet but little part in the affairs of state, but they were enfranchised voters, and the position they were beginning to assume in mercantile circles was giving them an influence which was too frequently underestimated. Though the more lawless class in the colony was still numerous and powerful, and its influence in behalf of the pirates hard to overcome, the better element was slowly but surely asserting its supremacy. The men to whom the enforcement of the laws was intrusted were no longer of the degraded type of Robert Quarry and his lieutenants of twenty years before. They were Englishmen with a pride in England and in the good name of her colonies, and the taunts of the Spaniards that Carolina was the nursery of lawlessness in America were not lost upon them. Their best efforts were put forth to redeem the honor of the Province, and after many years of toil and danger, they witnessed the triumph of their influence, which had so long seemed barren and hopeless. With the new period Carolina entered upon a new life, and when the eighteenth century dawned, the piracies which had ruined the commerce of some of the richest dependencies of England, were a thing of the past, and the colonies—especially those in the South— for more than ten years enjoyed an immunity from depredation such as had not been known since the foundation of the English Plantations in America. During the first years of the new century Charles Town, which had been the harbor for the greatest desperadoes of the western world, strung up pirates at the entrance of the port, scarcely waiting to hurry through the formality of a trial. The Province was able of itself to drive from the coast any outlaw who, more daring than the rest, might show his colors in those waters; and it was not until nearly two decades later that the continued Indian wars so depleted the strength of the colony that the pirates again overran the coast, laid the city under tribute, and for the second time succeeded in accomplishing almost the complete wreck of English commerce in the new world.

In noting the improvement in the moral condition of Carolina during the last years of the seventeenth century, we cannot lose sight of the Fundamental Constitutions of the Province. Much of the turmoil and lawlessness had been directly traceable to the operation, or rather the failure of the operation, of this utopian code, which the Proprietors insisted on enforcing in almost every impracticable detail. In 1693, during the administration of Ludwell, these Constitutions, which had been framed by the great philosopher Locke, to

be " the sacred and unalterable form and .rule of government of Carolina forever," were to all intents and purposes
abrogated.[1] This abrogation marks the turning-point in
Carolina's early history. Although little immediate improvement was to be noted, the colony was placed in a position where reform could be worked out successfully. The
influences which tended to a better condition of affairs could
now have freer play, and nowhere did they manifest themselves so strongly as in the reaction against the pirates,
which, as we have seen, commenced within a twelvemonth,
and produced definite results even during the unsuccessful
administration of Thomas Smith; and when Archdale appeared two years later, the people were prepared for the
establishment of a government which should continue for
many years prosperous and without reproach. The charter
and their own statutes were all that they needed to maintain
a strong and wholesome rule; and when in 1698 the Proprietors attempted to foist a revised set of the Constitutions
on them, they asserted their charter rights, and utterly rejected the code.[2]

Another circumstance of much less importance, but
which contributed greatly to allaying the irritation of the
public mind, was the order of the Proprietors, made during
Smith's administration, to the effect that legislative bills
should be permitted to originate in the Commons, as well as
in the Upper House of the Assembly.[3] This precluded the
possibility of a recurrence of such a legislative deadlock as
was witnessed in the time of Colleton, and gave great satisfaction to the people. From this time on, the popular
House of the Assembly exercised the privileges and usages
of the British House of Commons, which have been continued to the present day with but little modification.

---

[1] Winsor, Vol. V., p. 313.

[2] The formal rejection of the Constitutions by South Carolina was
not until Sept. 1st, 1702. See 1 S. C. Stats., p. 42.

[3] See S. C. Commons House Journals, May 15th, 1694.

CHAPTER III.

In the preceding chapters the name Carolina has been used to designate all that territory owned by the Lords Proprietors which lay between Virginia and what was afterwards the colony of Georgia, although at one time three distinct governments existed within those limits: one at Albemarle, one at Cape Fear, and one at Charles Town. The terms "North" and "South" as applied to the divisions of the Province did not come into common use until about 1690, and before that time it was impossible to know to what part of the Province the charges of harboring pirates could be directly laid. "South Carolina" appears for the first time in the records in January, 1685.[1] It is first used in the statutes in 1696,[2] although it was not until 1729 that the two colonies were formally separated.

It was during the last decade of the seventeenth century that the part of the Province corresponding to the present State of North Carolina began to attract particular attention as a resort for pirates. Although it was an older colony than "Carolina south and west of Cape Feare," as the old documents described South Carolina, during its early days it was in a certain way subordinate to the southern portion of the Province. For many years it was nominally ruled "by a deputy commissioned by the Governor of South Carolina,"[3] although, to quote an old authority, "every one

---

[1] MS. Grant Book G, S. C. Sec. of State's Office, p. 185.

[2] 2 S. C. Stat., p. 124. "North Carolina" appears in the Va. Council Proceedings in 1689. See N. C. Col. Rec., Vol. I., p. 357.

[3] Spotswood's Letters, Vol. I., p. 81. See *Ibid.*, p. 91, for reference to appointments of Thos. Carey and Edw. Hyde. See also Winsor, Vol. V., pp. 296-97.

did what was right in his own eyes, paying tribute neither to God nor to Caesar."[1] It was a country, wrote Governor Spotswood, "where there's scarce any form of government,"[2] and it is not surprising that the outlaws of that time found it a safe and pleasant refuge. "The common sanctuary of runaways" it had been styled,[3] and during all the turbulent years of the Proprietary government it had vied with many other English colonies in America in encouraging the pirates to frequent its coasts. As early as the year 1696 Edward Randolph reported that "pyrats and runaway servants resort to this place,"[4] and by 1700, during which year the same officer sent several reports to England, it had fully established its reputation as "a place which receives pirates, runaways and illegal traders."[5]

North Carolina, however, had not always been thus. When William Edmundson, the Quaker, visited it about twenty years after its settlement, "he met with a tender people,"[6] who lived in humble content along the banks of their noble rivers, and pursued their pastoral occupations in a state of almost Arcadian civilization. But numerous causes, more or less clearly defined by the earlier chroniclers,

---

[1] Byrd MS., ed. 1841, p. 32.

[2] Spotswood, Vol. I., p. 35.

[3] *Ibid.*, p. 108. According to Dr. S. B. Weeks in "The Religious Development in the Province of North Carolina," (J. H. U. Hist. and Polit. Studies, 10th series, V-VI., p. 49) Spotswood was "always notoriously unjust when writing of North Carolina affairs," but in the present instance he was eminently correct. Dr. Weeks himself says the colony had lapsed "into a state but one degree better than barbarism." (*Ibid.*, p. 8). In regard to Spotswood's injustice to N. C., a very careful reading of his letters fails to disclose it to the present writer, and his strictures on that government are freely corroborated by other authorities. Spotwood's actions when North Carolina needed his assistance would not seem to indicate that he was unduly prejudiced against the colony.

[4] S. C. Hist. Soc. Coll., Vol. II., p. 196.

[5] N. C. Colonial Records, Vol. I., p. 527.

[6] Fox's Journals, p. 453.

combined to work a change among them,[1] and by the beginning of the eighteenth century they had attained a by no means enviable reputation for harboring and dealing with the pirates who had now begun to make the numerous creeks and inlets of the coast their frequent resort. The North Carolinians had no such extensive maritime commerce as did the settlers at Charles Town, and were therefore seldom annoyed by the pirates infringing on their property rights.

To make matters worse, the authorities connived in a most shameless manner at the presence of these lawless freebooters, and they soon learned to know that they could come and go in North Carolina without hindrance. At a little later period " the Court of Admiralty was a regular sharper's shop,"[2] and there is no reason to believe that it was any purer during the time with which we are now dealing. The English authorities paid much less attention to this colony than to the one in South Carolina, and owing to the loose and indirect method of government, crimes could go unpunished in one settlement which would have met with swift and severe justice in the other. In South Carolina no one stood between the government and the Proprietors, the latter having a direct supervision over the affairs of the colony. Although the pirates were from time to time tolerated and encouraged, they could never consider the South Carolinians as friends who could be trusted. They knew not at what moment they might, at the order of the Proprietors, be apprehended and strung up in chains at the entrance of the port as a ghastly warning to evil-doers, as their companions had been treated on several occasions. In North Carolina they had no such apprehensions. The people were their friends, and the people were accustomed to treat the authority of their Governor with a contempt

---

[1] The imposition of the Fundamental Constitutions had as much to do with it as anything else.

[2] Hawks, Vol. II., p. 206.

which made it impossible for him to enforce an unpopular law. If a Governor was sent them who was so unfortunate as to possess a tender conscience, they did not hesitate to lock him in prison[1] and run the government to suit them-selves until they were given another by the South Carolina authorities.

The early history of North Carolina was sadly neglected by contemporary writers. " So carelessly has the history of North Carolina been written," says Bancroft, " that the name, the merits and the end of its first Governor were not known."[2] What little history we have of the early province makes scanty mention of piracy, presumably because the old historians found but little to say of it. The coast was thinly settled, and the outlaws could easily come and go among the people without causing any particular stir. Smuggling in those days was considered a legitimate occupation in all the colonies,[3] and when a vessel made her way up the rivers, past the customs officers, under the cover of night, no one took the trouble to inquire whether she was simply a con-traband trader, or whether she flew the black flag from her masthead when out of the reach of the law. There were many available harbors along the coast whose shores had never yet been disturbed by the ring of the settler's axe, and here amid the loneliness of the forest the pirates could beach and burn their prizes, and never a rumor of their invasions come to the ears of the king's officers.

How long this went on it is impossible to say. It had been a practice of many years standing when we first hear of it, and there can be no possible doubt that it was with the connivance of the colonists that it was permitted to grow into the evil that it soon became. The North Corolinians certainly took no steps to rid themselves of their lawless

---

[1] Spotswood's Letters, Vol. I., p. 108.

[2] Note in Bancroft, Vol. II., p. 135 (orig. edition). Also see *Ibid.*, p. 134.

[3] As a result of the Navigation Acts. See above, pp. 17-19.

visitors, but following the example of their brother-settlers at Charles Town, did much to encourage them. It was not until the constant presence of the pirates in North Carolina became a source of great annoyance, if not of great danger, to the neighboring colonies, that any particular notice was taken of them, and even then we have few, if any, detailed and authentic accounts of their exploits. Complaints of their outrages became numerous, and frequent attention was called to the fact that they found a safe shelter from justice among the inhabitants of this turbulent colony. Evidently reliable testimony was hard to secure, and as only vague and general charges could be preferred, the commands of the Lords Proprietors to their Governors and Councils could only be of the most general nature,—so general, in fact, that nobody deemed it his duty to see that they were complied with.

Such was the situation in North Carolina at the end of the seventeenth century, and we have no reason to believe that the conditions were improved until very many years later. What was wanted was a strong power at the head of the government, and this was not enjoyed until the Proprietary rule was overthrown, and the Crown assumed direct charge of affairs.

From this picture we turn to view the situation which was about to be presented in South Carolina. It is indeed with a grateful sense of relief that the historian emerges from the misty years of the seventeenth century into the brighter light of the earlier decades of the eighteenth. During the latter period not only does he find records sufficiently complete and authentic upon which to base a continuous historical narrative, but he learns, too, that the colony during that time was making history for itself which was well worth recording. During the first thirty years of her existence South Carolina had done little which she could with any pardonable pride wish to hand down to posterity; the colonists evidently considered themselves no more than a very insignificant part of a very great whole, and it was not unnatural that they made little, if any, effort to preserve their records. With the beginning of the new century, however, new ambitions began to enter into the life of the people. The colony had donned a robe of dignity, and some of her far-seeing, though obscure, statesmen began to realize that her career could, and should, be made long and honorable. We find a greater care exercised in the preservation of records, some feeble attempts to write her history, brief and unsatisfactory as it had been, and a little later one settler took so much interest in her political organization as to prepare an elaborate study of her whole governmental economy.[1] It is therefore with a feeling of satisfaction that we enter upon this new period, for henceforth we find the history of the colony an honorable one. True, it was torn by factional strife, but when was South Carolina ever other than turbulent? But this party warfare, the clash of Churchmen and Dissenters, and the wrangling of the people and the Proprietors over their alleged respective rights, do not seem to have had any immediate effect on the prosperity of the settlement. For more than ten years after the wholesome administration of Governor James Moore, the colony at Charles Town grew and prospered. The agricultural staples of the Province were in an increasing demand, and not only was Carolina rice quoted high in the markets of England, but the great timber tracts, which even to this day are far from being exhausted, supplied spars and masts for the Royal Navy, while the bounty placed upon naval stores in 1703 in hopes of breaking the Swedish monopoly,[2] had built up a great trade in that branch of exporting. The laws against piracy were so severe, and the determination of the government to enforce them so fixed, that the freebooters were scarcely heard of along the coast, although they continued to be a scourge to New England and the Northern colonies

---

[1] See Note 1, p. 98.

[2] Cunningham's Growth of English Industry and Commerce, (1892), p. 285.

for many years later.[1] None of the Carolina records mentions them during these years, and it is quite evident that between the action of the South Carolina authorities and that of the English government, they were very generally driven out.[2]

In 1712, while Deputy Governor Hyde was striving to heal the dissensions which had recently torn North Carolina asunder, the South Carolina Assembly passed an omnibus bill which ordered the enforcement of the English pirate law along with many other laws of the mother-country which it was thought well to promulgate in the colony.[3] It is not known that there was any special reason for the passage of this law at this time. It is probable that it was passed simply as a measure of precaution, along with many other statutes of the realm which were thought to be applicable to conditions which might arise in the colony at any time. It is worth mentioning, however, that in October of the same year Governor Spotswood had written to the Council of Trade from Virginia that " the fear of Enemys by Sea (except that of Pyrates), are now happily removed by the peace."[4] No doubt, at this time, as at many others, there were rumors in the air about pirate incursions, but they were not sufficiently grave to give any real cause for alarm. The rumors continued, however, and came to the ears of the British government, which was the occasion of Spotswood writing late in the succeeding year (December, 1713) that he was " of the opinion that the Ship already here is Sufficient, and that there's no occasion to put her Majesty to a further Expence untill it appears that ye Pyrates are more formidable than there's yet any reason to apprehend they are."[5]

---

[1] See 5 Mass. Hist. Coll., Vol. VI., pp. 109, 110 (Sewall's Journal).

[2] In the N. C. Col. Rec., Vol. I., p. 674, is a reference to pirates frequenting the N. C. coast. The date of this paper is 1707, but there is reason to suppose that the reference had regard only to times past.

[3] S. C. Stats., Vol. II., p. 470.

[4] Spotswood's Letters, Vol. II., p. 2.   [5] *Ibid.*, p. 45.

But despite Spotswood's protestations that the coast was in no danger, the South Carolina Assembly showed its wisdom by passing the anti-pirate law, and subsequent events proved that it was done none too soon.   Even before the Assembly which enacted it was convened, clouds of disaster were hovering over the colony, portending a storm which was to last for years, and which was destined to expend itself in blood and revolution.

Late in the summer of 1711 the North Carolinians had some contention with the Tuscarora Indians, which on September 22d culminated in a fearful massacre of the whites.[1] South Carolina was appealed to for aid, and the troops sent out under Colonel John Barnwell succeeded in bringing the savages to terms after punishing them severely.   In a few months, however, another fierce outbreak occurred, and South Carolina was again called upon to assist in suppressing it.   It was not long before it became evident that the fires of insurrection had been kindled along the entire border, and South Carolina soon had as much as she could attend to in keeping down the savage tribes within her own limits.   Cut off by six hundred miles of wilderness from the nearest strong colony, Virginia, she could not enjoy the benefits of co-operation with other settlements as could the colonies further north, but was thrown absolutely on her own resources for protection.   At first these were very considerable, but continued heavy appropriations to meet the expenses of the war depleted the treasury, and by 1715 the Province was in a thoroughly exhausted condition.   Many of the inhabitants had been slaughtered, and the planters had been compelled to flee from the outlying plantations to the protection of the town.   The result was that few crops were planted for several successive years, and as the agricultural and farm products were the chief source of revenue, money and supplies became scarce, and the colonists found themselves in a position where ruin stared them in the face.

---

[1] Spotswood's Letters, Vol. I., p. 118.

The Indians, recognizing their great inferiority to the whites, refused to meet them in a decisive battle, but resorted to bush-fighting and night-raiding, which made it necessary to keep a standing army in a continual state of organization, which was a great expense to the already impoverished colony.

In these trying times South Carolina found a friend indeed worth having in Lieutenant-Governor Spotswood of Virginia. Scarcely had this generous official heard of the condition of the colony than he took steps toward rendering them substantial assistance. He not only ordered the war-ship stationed on the Virginia coast to proceed immediately to Charles Town " to keep open the Communication with the Town," but " writt to ye Govern'rs to the Northward advising them to send likewise his Maj'ty's Ships in those Stations to visit y't place from time to time."[1]

This prompt offer of aid incited the South Carolinians to apply directly to Virginia for assistance in putting down the savages, and commissioners were sent to Williamsburg to ask for both men and arms. The response was characteristic of the people of the Old Dominion. Within fifteen days the envoys sailed back to Charles Town with one hundred and eighteen Virginia volunteers, and between forty and fifty more sailed a few days later.[2] By utilizing these auxiliary troops Governor Craven succeeded in forcing the Indians to at least an armed peace, although not until the entire country, to within twenty-five or thirty miles of Charleston, had been devastated.[3]

In the midst of all these hardships, when the colonists were almost ready to abandon their homes and estates, a still greater misfortune assailed them. Whatever their troubles with their savage neighbors had been, for years past the

---

[1] Spotswood's Letters, Vol. II., p. 112.

[2] *Ibid.*, p. 119. See *Ibid.*, pp. 131-132, 135-136, for account of the ill-treatment of the Virginians by S. Carolina.

[3] *Ibid.*, p. 121.

commerce of the Province had been unobstructed by sea.
Their produce, however small the quantity, had for a long
time been delivered in the markets of England without any
interference from their old enemies the pirates, and since all
internal commerce had been destroyed by the Indians, the
Carolinians now had nothing on which to depend save the
trade with the mother-country. One can therefore easily
imagine the consternation with which they received repeated
rumors that the freebooters were beginning to reappear on
the coast in no inconsiderable force. Frightened by the
stringent provincial laws, they had years before retreated to
their strongholds in the West Indies, but now that the
South Carolinians were compelled to keep all their forces on
the frontier, and were unable to punish the trespassers by
sea, the pirates returned, and with their numbers greatly increased by the accession of many of the privateers which had
been thrown out of employment by the recent peace of
Utrecht, in a few months were a far greater menace than
they had ever been at any previous time. They settled
themselves at New Providence, in the Bahamas, and at Cape
Fear, in North Carolina,[1] from whence they issued on their
lawless excursions, diffusing the terror of their names along
the entire North American coasts. James Logan, Secretary
of Pennsylvania, is authority for the statement that there
were in 1717 fifteen hundred pirates on the coast, eight hundred of whom had their headquarters at New Providence.[2]
From timid and occasional ventures, they soon entered upon
enterprises of the utmost boldness and audacity. Many of
them combined together, and for five years they maintained
themselves as the invincible masters of the Gulf of Florida
and all adjacent waters, preying without distinction on the
commerce of every nation whose flag was found upon the
seas of the new world. They swept the coasts from New
Foundland to South America, plundering their prizes at

---

[1] Hawks, Vol. II., p. 272.
[2] Watson Annals, Vol. II., p. 218.

sea, or carrying them into Cape Fear or New Providence, as best suited their convenience.

For several years the South Carolinians, distracted by internal wars and dissensions, were too weak to strike a single blow in their own defense, and the pirates had the freest range along their coasts. In 1715 many captures were made, and it became evident that unless some immediate action were taken the commerce of the colony would be annihilated. Already had petitions for assistance been sent to England by both the South Carolina and the Virginia authorities,[1] but they were ignored, and the Proprietors were now earnestly entreated to give their suffering subjects some relief. The London agent of the colony, Abel Kettleby,[2] waited on their Lordships[3] and laid before them the pressing needs of the Province, but the reply given was most unsatisfactory. Evidently the Proprietors had lost interest in their American possessions, and did not propose to make any further outlay of money to keep up an investment which at best had been a disastrous one. But the energetic agent was not at the end of his resources. The affair was too serious to be made subject solely to the selfish action of the Proprietors. Englishmen, loyal subjects of the Crown, had been induced to go to Carolina by fair representations of the advantages of the country, and they could not now be left to perish in the wilderness without one effort being made to save them. All these arguments the agent doubtless presented to the Proprietors, but without effect, and he therefore boldly petitioned the House of Commons to interfere in behalf of their perishing fellow-countrymen in America. The Commons took the matter up without delay, and addressing the king, begged that relief should be given the colony immediately. George I. referred the matter to the

---

[1] Spotswood's Letters, Vol. II., pp. 168, 169.

[2] Kettleby had been created a Landgrave in 1709. His patent, indited in Latin, is in the London State Paper Office. See S. C. Hist. Soc. Coll., Vol. I., p. 155.

[3] Hewat in Carroll, Vol. I., p. 200.

Lords Commissioners of Trade and Plantations, who decided that the government could do nothing unless the Proprietors vested the colony in the Crown.[1] On July 6th, 1715, the attention of the Proprietors was brought to this action, and two days later Lord Carteret addressed a letter to the trade commissioners, in which he made the following statement: " We, the Proprietors of Carolina, having met on this melancholy occasion, to our great grief find that we are utterly unable of ourselves to afford our colony suitable assistance in this conjuncture, and unless his Majesty will graciously please to interpose, we can foresee nothing but the utter destruction of his Majesty's faithful subjects in those parts."[2] After this confession it would seem that the Crown would have immediately assumed charge of the affairs of the Province, and have rendered the much-needed assistance, but no such event is to be recorded. We must not forget that England, in common with all the countries of Europe, viewed her colonies only as estates which were to be worked for the benefit of the mother-country, and that the economic school of that time taught her statesmen to consider the colonial trade only as a means toward increasing the public revenue. Maintaining such views, it is not surprising that the English government was unwilling to assume the responsibility of a Province which would prove nothing but an expense and a constant annoyance to the Board of Trade. It was much easier to force the Proprietors to continue their responsibility, and to hold them amenable for any complications that might arise. So other matters were allowed to push Carolina's grievances aside. Much correspondence ensued between the different

---

[1] Hewat in Carroll, Vol. I., p. 201.

[2] N. C. Col. Rec., Vol. II., p. 188. See Yonge's Narrative in Carroll, Vol. II., p. 162, for an account of the manner in which the Proprietors conducted the business of the colony. It is not remarkable, after their wanton neglect, that they were unable to do anything for their subjects.

branches of the government, but it all ended in the colonists being left to take care of themselves as best they could.[1]

For more than thirty years previous to this time the Vice-Admiralty Court of the Province had been in an imperfect state of organization, owing largely to the fact that its jurisdiction had never been clearly defined.[2] It was a matter of serious doubt as to the source of its authority, and it was sometimes allowed to act, and sometimes ordered to stay its hand. Conflicting orders were constantly being transmitted to the Governor. First, he would be ordered to try all pirates in the provincial courts, and probably the very next ship would bring instructions to hold all such prisoners at the king's pleasure, or to send them to England to be tried before the Lord Admiral. But in 1716 the crimes over which the Admiral had jurisdiction increased so greatly in Carolina that a reorganization of the court became an imperative necessity. The indifference of the home government seems to have discouraged any thought of seeking the right to organize the court from the proper source, and in the summer of this year Lord Carteret, the Palatine, or President of the Board of Proprietors, issued a warrant to Nicholas Trott, the Chief Justice of the Province, authorizing him to sit as Judge of the Vice-Admiralty Court.[3] It is by no means clear what right the Proprietors, even when acting as a board, had to appoint judges in admiralty, and had the matter been investigated it is highly probable that this act of a single Proprietor would have been shown to be an undoubted usurpation of power. But England at this time was bestowing very little attention upon her colonies, and

---

[1] See N. C. Col. Rec., Vol. II., p. 190, for Caleb Heathcote's account of the condition of affairs in Charles Town.

[2] The act of March, 1701, "For the better Regulating the Proceedings of the Court of Admiralty, etc.," applied only to the civil side of the Court. See 2 S. C. Stats., p. 167. It was repealed in May, 1703 (*Ibid.*, p. 214), and not again revived, although some of the usages of the English Adm. Courts were put in force by the omnibus act of 1712 (*Ibid.*, p. 401 *sqq.*).

[3] Hewat in Carroll, Vol. I., p. 206.

Trott did not let the cloud which might have been thrown upon his title deter him from speedily assuming his new dignity. His chief characteristic was a greed for power, and he was very prompt in the present instance to accept the additional trust which had been assigned him. The first record of his court of Vice-Admiralty is dated November 13th, 1716, which must have been very soon after his commission arrived out from England. Captain Nathaniel Partridge appeared as Provost-Marshal, and John Wallis, Gent., as " Register," or clerk.[1]

Whatever may have been Trott's faults—and he had many —he was a terror to all evil-doers who fell into his hands, and the fact that he presided over the court was a guarantee that no guilty man would escape. Encouraged by these circumstances, and having at last rid themselves of their Indian enemies, the colonists now turned their attention to bringing the pirates to justice. Their resources were exhausted, but this did not deter them from making earnest and repeated efforts. How and by whom the first captures were made, history does not relate, but at the sitting of the court on November 27, the grand jury returned indictments for piracy against nine men who were charged with seizing the sloop Providence, owned by William Gibson and Andrew Allen, two Charleston merchants, on August 2d, 1716. Judge Trott presided, assisted by the following persons who had received special commissions from England for this duty: " the Hon'ble Captain Thomas Howard, commander of his Majesty's ship, the Shorham; the Hon'ble Charles Hart, Esqr., one of the members of Our Council in South Carolina; the Hon'ble Coll. Thomas Broughton, Speaker of the Lower House of Assembly in South Carolina; Arthur Middleton and Ralph Izard, Esqrs.; Captain Philip Dawes; Capt. Will'm Cuthbert, Commander of the Fortune Frigate; Capt. Allen Archer, Commander of the Brigantine Experiment; and Samuel Deane and Edward Brailsford, Merchts."[2]

---

[1] S. C. Admiralty Court Records, Book A and B.
[2] *Ibid.*

The fact that this trial resulted in a verdict of not guilty did not deter the colonists from continuing their efforts to stamp out the scourge. In April, 1717, the Province was further alarmed by news of activity on the part of the pirates in the West Indies, and it being probable that the Shorham, the war vessel stationed at Charles Town, would shortly be ordered elsewhere, the Commons House of the Assembly presented the following address to Deputy Governor Daniel and his Council:

" May it please your Honors: As this House has received information that the Governor of St. Augustine having advice and intelligance sent from the Governor of the Havanna, to be upon his gourd, by reason of the design the Pirates at the Bahama Islands (and who are numerous) have to attack them; and as we cannot suppose, that any such persons have a regard to, or make any difference or distinction, between the people of any nation whatsoever; we ought to provide for the safty and defence of the Inhabitants of this Province, whom we are chosen for and sit here to represent; and as this House humbly conceives; that it would be requisite to address Capt. Howard, Commander of his Magesty Ship Shorum to desire him to stay some time longer here with his said Ship; and that it would in some measure deter the Pirates from coming here, while they know that a King's ship does tarry among us; We therefore desire your Honors, to appoint a committee of your House, to join a committee of ours, in a conference to draw up the said address to Capt. Howard in case the same be agreed upon at the conference, which we desire may be where, and as soon as you shall think fit to appoint.

GEORGE LOGAN, Speaker."[1]

This proposition was not acceded to by Daniel and his Council, and the Shorham sailed away to Virginia, with

---

[1] S. C. Commons House Journals, No. 5, p. 258 (dated April 17th, 1717).

orders to proceed without delay to England,[1] just at the time when there was most urgent need for her presence on the coast.

But despite their depleted resources and their unprotected state, the colonists were active, and in June, 1717, the Vice-Admiralty Court was again convened, and four pirates, who had been recently taken, were placed on trial for their lives. Stephen James De Cossey, Francis De Mont, Francis Rossoe, and Emanuel Ernandos were convicted of piratically taking the vessels, the Turtle Dove, the Penelope, and the Virgin Queen, in July of the previous year, and having been sentenced to death by Judge Trott, were promptly executed at the hands of the law.[2]

The trials last mentioned were held during the first year of the administration of Governor Robert Johnson, and were the results of the first of a series of operations conducted by that able official, which resulted in the final extermination of piracy as a crime in the Carolinas. Johnson had been commissioned Governor in April, 1717, and no man could have entered upon office under more inauspicious circumstances. The Province was in a deplorable condition, and so serious had the situation become that the inhabitants had already directed a petition to the king, praying to be taken directly under the royal protection. Their repeated complaints to the Proprietors had been either ignored or reproved as the outgrowth of an unruly and factional spirit.[3] The Indian wars had caused the ruin of the planters, and commerce had been almost annihilated by the hordes of pirates who now boldly threw the black flag to the winds of every sea. They had actually colonized the island of New Providence, and for several years had been permitted free access to the Cape Fear and other rivers and inlets of the North Carolina coast, from whence they issued

---

[1] Spotswood Letters, Vol. II., p. 246.
[2] S. C. Adm. Court Records, Book A and B.
[3] Rivers, 277.

on lawless cruises, and to which they could retire in security on the first indication of danger.

But the colonies were not to be wholly abandoned to the mercy of their enemies. Although their petitions were ignored with distressing regularity, they had friends who were much nearer to the throne than their agents, who now stepped in with demands which the king could not afford to ignore. In London there was a large and influential class of merchants who had grown rich in the trade with the New World, and it was with no great equanimity of mind that they saw their business being destroyed by the lawless hand of the pirates. They accordingly combined with the masters of their vessels and petitioned the king in council, showing how the trade had been demoralized, and praying for relief.[1] George I. was about this time engaging the power of the British navy in the Baltic in his endeavors to protect his little German Electorate against the threatened movements of Charles XII. of Sweden,[2] and as no vessels were available for the American coast he resorted to a most ignominious expediency. Thinking that some of the pirates might wish to leave off their lawless lives, and that the number could be much reduced if general indemnity were granted, he declared an act of grace which guaranteed a full pardon to all who would surrender to some competent official within twelve months, and take an oath of allegiance and fealty to the Crown. It was not the first time that an English sovereign had resorted to this questionable method of disposing of a special class of criminals, but on this occasion the plan was by no means successful. The pirates were too secure in their lawlessness to leave off their criminal practices when no other inducement than a pardon for past offenses was offered. Governor Johnson did his duty, however. The king's proclamation was published throughout Carolina, and in his zeal to further his Majesty's service he was inclined to

---

[1] Hewat, in Carroll, Vol. I., pp. 208-209.

[2] Green, Hist. of the English People, Book VIII., Chap. IV.

go beyond his jurisdiction in extending the offer of pardon. On December 3rd, 1717, in a written message to the Commons House, he made a proposition looking to the reclamation of all Carolinians who had become pirates with their headquarters in other parts of America.

"His Majesty," he said, "being pleased to issue out his Royal Proclamation, extending his pardon to all pirates, that shall lay hold on the same, and surrendering themselves according to the time limited in said proclamation; and we having several of our inhabitants, that unwarily and without due consideration, have engaged in that ill course of life, and are now resident at the Bahama Islands, and other places adjacent, I think it a duty incumbent on me, with all speed to send his Majesty's proclamation thither, to let our people see, that they may return hither again in safety to us, if in time they embrace his Majesty's royal favor; therefore some proper person must be thought of to carry this proclamation to them; and Col. Parris being willing to undertake the same (who is very well known to all the inhabitants of this Province) if you can spare him from the Public business; I shall give him my instructions accordingly."[1]

There is no record that Colonel Parris ever went to the Bahamas, or elsewhere, to promulgate the king's proclamation, and it is probable that the pirates were left to learn of his Majesty's leniency as best they could. It is certain that the Carolinians who had entered upon this "ill course of life" had not done so as "unwarily and without due consideration" as Governor Johnson seemed to think. If they had, there is no doubt that they considered it more carefully afterwards, and concluded they had done quite the right thing. Some few came in to the officials and took the oath, but they were soon back at their old habits,[2] while the great majority of them ignored the offer, and took renewed advantage of every opportunity to plunder the king's commerce, and render the coast dangerous for every kind of craft save an armed ship-of-war.

---

[1] S. C. Commons House Journals, No. 5, p. 388.

[2] S. C. Hist. Soc. Coll., Vol. II., p. 257.

Although no armament was available at this time for the protection of Carolina, such pressure was brought to bear on the king that Captain Woodes Rogers was dispatched with several small vessels against New Providence, with instructions to exterminate the pirates in that quarter, and establish a regular government in the island. Rogers arrived at New Providence in July, 1718, and took possession of the colony for the Crown. He found a large number of pirates there, all of whom surrendered and took the oath, except Charles Vane, who pursued a more desperate course. When he heard that Rogers had arrived off the bar, he wrote him a letter offering to surrender on the condition that he would be permitted to dispose of what spoil he had in the manner that suited himself. Receiving no assurances from Rogers, he determined to escape, and attempted to cross the bar. He was met by two of the invading vessels, with whom he exchanged shots, and after several exciting adventures, succeeded in getting safely to sea with ninety men, in a sloop belonging to one of his officers named Yeates, and made for the Carolina coast, where he engaged in several piratical exploits.[1]

Many of the outlaws who were at New Providence surrendered to the new Governor, and in a short time Rogers succeeded in establishing a law-abiding and prosperous colony. But this action on the part of the English authorities, while it did much to relieve the West Indies, greatly aggravated the situation in both North and South Carolina. Finding themselves driven out from New Providence and the Bahamas generally, they had no other convenient rendezvous besides the North Carolina coast, and before many months had passed, they swarmed into the Cape Fear and Pamlico rivers in greater numbers than the government of that weak Province could possibly cope with. How they were expelled from this their last stronghold on the American coast will form the subject of the succeeding chapters.

---

[1] Johnson's History of the Pirates (Edition 1726), Vol. I., p. 142 *et seq.*

CHAPTER IV.

While Rogers was on his voyage to New Providence, South Carolina found herself in most distressing straits, and was compelled to submit to the most humiliating insults and outrages from the pirates of the North Carolina coast.

Early in June Edward Thatch,[1] who under the sobriquet of " Black-Beard " had spread terror along the entire North American coast, suddenly appeared off Charles Town with a powerful equipment, and began a series of most flagrant outrages. Thatch had for some time made Ocracoke Inlet, on the North Carolina coast, his chief resort, and " Thatch's Hole," an old landing in that vicinity for many years after his day, recalled to the mariner the time when it was as much as his life was worth for a skipper to venture into those waters unless heavily armed and ready for a desperate fight. When the proclamation of George I. was issued, Thatch and his crew went in to Governor Eden of North Carolina, and in January, 1718, surrendered and took the oath.[2] His men scattered themselves through the country, many of them going north to Pennsylvania. Thatch lingered about his old haunts, but erelong the temptations of the old free life proved too strong for him. Before the end of the winter he was again fitted out from North Carolina, and was once

---

[1] Also spelled Teach. Watson says in his Annals, Vol. II., p. 220: "I happened to know the fact that Blackbeard, whose family name was given as Teach, was in reality named Drummond, a native of Bristol. I have learned this fact from one of his family and name, of respectable standing in Virginia, near Hampton." I have adopted the spelling of the name used in the contemporary court records. See Howell's State Trials, Trials of Bonnet et al., Vol. XV.

[2] See Pollock's Letter Book, N. C. Col. Rec., Vol. II., pp. 318-20.

more harrying the coast and capturing vessels of all nationalities. It was during one of these cruises that he visited the Bay of Honduras, where he met Stede Bonnet, late of Barbadoes, and the two returned to Carolina together, taking numerous prizes by the way. Many of the mariners on board the captured vessels entered into the pirate compact, and by the time Thatch reached the South Carolina coast he was in command of a fleet consisting of a ship of more than 40 guns and three attendant sloops, on board of which were above 400 men.[1]

Thatch felt himself strong enough to defy the government, and dropping anchor in front of Charles Town, he commenced operations by capturing the pilot-boat which was stationed on the bar, and within a few days took no less than eight or nine outward-bound vessels.[2] Among these captures was a ship bound for London, carrying a number of Carolina passengers, including Samuel Wragg, a member of the Council of the Province. How the pirates became aware that they had made so distinguished a prisoner is not known, but having ascertained the fact, they determined to make the best of their good fortune. At this time the fleet was in need of certain medicines, and Thatch had his surgeon prepare a list of the desired articles, and proceeded to demand them of Governor Johnson. Arming a boat, he sent it up to the city in command of one of his officers named Richards. The latter was accompanied by two other pirates, and by a Mr. Marks, a citizen of Charles Town, who was ordered to lay the situation before the Governor, and to inform him that if the necessary supplies were not immediately forthcoming, and the men permitted to return unharmed, the heads of Mr. Wragg and the other Charles Town prisoners would be sent in to him.[3]

---

[1] S. C. Hist. Soc. Coll., Vol. II., p. 236.

[2] *Ibid.*

[3] Weedin has unintentionally done Governor Johnson an injustice in mentioning this event. He says Thatch " prevailed over the Governor of S. C. so that he obtained a chest of much-needed medi-

Marks was given two days in which to accomplish his mission, and the prisoners, who had been acquainted with the demands and the attached condition, awaited with the most intense anxiety the return of the embassy. Two days passed and the party did not return. Thatch suspected that his men had been seized by the authorities, and notified Wragg that his entire party could prepare for immediate death. He was persuaded, however, to stay his bloody order for at least a day, and while awaiting the expiration of that time a message was received from Marks that their boat had been overturned by a squall, and that after many difficulties and much delay, they had succeeded in reaching Charles Town. This explanation satisfied Thatch and he gave the prisoners the freedom of the vessel until the third day, when, losing patience, he again swore that he would be revenged on the colony for the supposed arrest of his men, by putting Wragg and his fellow-voyagers to an instant death. The prisoners, to save themselves, then offered a desperate condition. Begging for a further reprieve, they agreed to pilot the pirate fleet into the harbor, and assist Thatch in battering down the defenseless town, in the event that proof was brought of the detention of the messengers by the authorities.[1] Nothing would have pleased the pirate chief better than to take so signal a vengeance for what he termed the treachery of the government, and he accordingly acceded to the proposition of the Carolinians and granted a further stay of the execution.

In the meantime Charles Town was in a state of desperation such as had never been known in all its turbulent history. Marks had laid Thatch's demands before the Governor, who recognized the case as one which would require

---

cines worth £300 or £400 with provisions for his vessels " (pp. 563-64). The connection in which this statement is made would lead the uninformed reader to suppose Johnson to have been in collusion with Thatch.

[1] Johnson is authority for this statement, but it is not possible to believe that Wragg was a party to the agreement.

the most delicate handling.   No time was to be lost; what was done must be done quickly.   Although a man of far more than ordinary ability, Johnson decided not to trust his own judgment in the matter, and convening his Council, he laid the situation before it.   The members realized that but one course was open to them; the pirates had them at the greatest disadvantage, and the only thing feasible was to accede to their insolent demands, and, if possible, seek to punish their audacity later.   The colony was in no condition to repel the invasion at this time.   The harbor was wholly unprotected, and there was not an armed vessel within hundreds of miles.   The Indian wars had bankrupted the treasury, and it was impossible to arm any of the merchant vessels in the harbor for a movement against the blockading fleet.

In the meantime Richards and his men were parading themselves up and down the principal streets, and their impudent behavior aroused the indignation of the people to the highest pitch.   This state of affairs was fraught with the greatest danger, as it was not known at what moment the pirates would be attacked by the infuriated populace, and such action would not only be the death-warrant of Thatch's prisoners, but would in all probability bring the guns of the pirate fleet to bear on the defenseless city.

The action of the Council was as prompt as the exigencies of the occasion demanded.   The medicines were prepared without delay, and in a few hours Marks, accompanied by his guard, was on his way to the bar.

His demands being satisfied, and a large quantity of rich spoil having been secured from the captured vessels, Thatch sent Wragg and the rest of the prisoners ashore in a half-naked condition.   After suffering numerous hardships they made their way back to Charles Town, glad to escape with their lives.[1]   Among Thatch's spoil were $6000 in specie which he took from Wragg.[2]

---

[1] The foregoing account of Thatch's exploits off Charles Town is made up partly from memoranda from MS. records in the London State Paper Office, and partly from Johnson's History.   The latter

Among the unfortunates who came so near falling victims to the bloody vengeance of Thatch on this occasion was William Wragg, a son of Samuel Wragg, who was at this time but four years of age, and who afterwards became one of the most distinguished men in the American colonies. He was educated in England, and held many responsible public positions in South Carolina during the period just prior to the Revolution. In 1771 he was tendered the Chief Justiceship of the Province, which he declined. He was a devoted loyalist during the struggle for independence, but such was his character that he retained the highest esteem of his fellow-countrymen. Foreseeing the success of the American arms, he disposed of his Carolina estates and in 1777 sailed for England. His vessel was lost on the coast of Holland in September of that year, and he was drowned with the entire crew. Such was the regard in which he was held that George III. had a memorial erected in Westminster Abbey in his honor.[3]

From Charles Town Thatch went to North Carolina, where he remained for some time in comparative idleness, and it was during this stay that he formed connections with the authorities of that colony which reflect as much dishonor upon its early history as the corrupt administration of Quarry did upon South Carolina thirty years before.

Charles Eden had been appointed Governor of North Carolina early in 1714, and was in charge of the government for eight years. The chief town of the colony was then Bath, in the present county of Beaufort. The country was

---

authority the author was inclined to doubt, but on comparing him in several instances with the MS. contemporary records, he was found to be remarkably accurate even in the minutest details. This leads to his being credited, although several seemingly improbable statements which could not be verified have been omitted. See also Howell's State Trials, Vol. XV., Trial of Bonnet et al.

[2] Hawks, Vol. II., p. 274.

[3] Ramsay, Vol. II., p. 532.

thinly settled, and Eden entered upon his office with very large ideas of progress, and could have advanced the prosperity of the colony most materially had he set about it in the right way. North Carolina was then divided into two customs districts, Currituck and Roanoke,[1] but the arrangement was not convenient, and in August, 1716, the Lords Proprietors, on a petition from Eden, constituted Bath a port of entry.[2] This might have indicated an increase of North Carolina's commerce, but whatever the condition was, Governor Eden, during the two years he had been in power, had not succeeded in strengthening the government.[3] The colony had been much reduced by Indian wars, and when Eden assumed power, the pirates had already taken possession of the coast, and there is no record of any attempt being made to drive them out. When Rogers established his government at New Providence they had no other convenient rendezvous than the North Carolina coast, and before many months they came into the Cape Fear and Pamlico rivers in greater numbers than had ever been known before.

Although some of these pirates were men whose names had inspired terror throughout half the world, to Thatch was awarded the distinction of being the most desperate of them all. On returning from Charles Town he disbanded his company, retaining for himself and a few chosen companions a small sloop, which he fitted out for an alleged trading expedition to the island of St. Thomas.[4] In a few weeks, however, he returned to Bath with a large French vessel, loaded with sugar and other merchandise, and going in to the Governor he made an affidavit that he had found it

---

[1] N. C. Colonial Records, Vol. II., p. vi.

[2] *Ibid.*

[3] See N. C. Colonial Records, Vol. II., preface, for a statement concerning the weakness of the government.

[4] Although given by several authorities, there is much doubt as to this point. Bonnet undoubtedly cleared for St. Thomas when he took the oath, and it is highly probable that the authorities have confused the two men. See Note 2, p. 90.

abandoned at sea.[1] "Strange ideas were entertained in those days of Admiralty jurisdiction,"[2] and Tobias Knight, the collector of the port, sitting as Vice-Admiralty Judge,[3] condemned the French vessel as a legitimate prize, and permitted Thatch to land the cargo and retain it for his own use. The pirate thereupon discharged the goods, and instead of selling the vessel, which was a valuable one, in order to cover up all traces of his crime, beached her on the coast some little distance from Bath, and burned her.

It was chiefly in connection with this prize that the names of Eden and Knight have been handed down in history besmirched with as much infamy as that which attaches to those of Fletcher and Nicolls in New York, or Quarry in South Carolina. Thatch had for some time been living on terms of great intimacy with many of the principal inhabitants, and was by no means an infrequent visitor at Knight's residence. Being in favor with the officials, he enjoyed a perfect immunity from punishment for the various outrages he perpetrated from time to time on the coastwise shipping. Complaints to the proper authorities were of no avail, and the license he was granted soon made him so reckless and arrogant that he aroused the bitter enmity of many of the inhabitants of Bath and the surrounding country, who might otherwise have joined the authorities in conniving at his residence in the colony. His depredations were extended up the coast as far as Pennsylvania, and on his expeditions to the North he not infrequently made Philadelphia his headquarters. This fact soon became notorious, and in August, 1718, Governor William Keith reported to his Council that he had issued a warrant for his apprehension.[4] Thatch was too shrewd to be taken in any trap, however, and the warrant was never served.

---

[1] Spotswood's Letters, Vol. II., p. 317.

[2] Hawks, Vol. II., p. 206.

[3] *Ibid.*, pp. 205-206.

[4] Minutes of Provincial Council, Pa., Vol. III., p. 45.

The peculiar circumstances of the taking of a small trading vessel about this time seem to have led Thatch's enemies to look about for some means of ridding the country of his presence. Seeing his intimacy with the North Carolina officials, they realized that they would have to look elsewhere than to their own government for help. Naturally they would have turned to South Carolina, but that colony now had all she could do in attending to her own troubles, and it was useless to apply for assistance there. During recent troubles Governor Spotswood, of Virginia, had rendered the colony valuable services, and it was to him that the North Carolinians now applied for relief. The case of the French prize had by this time become notorious in the Province, and whatever Eden and Knight pretended to think of it, everybody knew it was a clear case of piracy, and that instead of attempting the apprehension of the miscreants, the authorities had connived at their crimes, and had, it was generally believed, been well paid for their connivance.

Affidavits setting forth these facts and the general circumstances were forwarded to Governor Spotswood, and " upon the repeated applications of the trading people " of North Carolina,[1] the Virginia Assembly offered a reward of £100 for the arrest of Thatch, £15 for the arrest of each of his officers, and £10 for each of his crew.[2] Not satisfied with simply offering a reward, however, Spotswood, deeming his own coasts in danger, determined to effect the immediate capture of Thatch and his crew. At this time two British war-vessels, the Lyme, Captain Ellis Brand, and the Pearl, were stationed in Hampton Roads, and Spotswood, hiring two sloops at his own expense,[3] equipped them and gave them in command of Captain Brand and Lieutenant Maynard, with instructions to repair to the North Carolina coast and bring Thatch and his crew to Virginia dead or alive.[4]

---

[1] Spotswood's Letters, Vol. II., p. 273.
[2] Hawks, Vol. II., p. 277.
[3] Spotswood's Letters, Vol. II., p. 305.
[4] The authorities are conflicting on the point of whether or not

The vessels being furnished with North Carolina pilots, they set sail about the middle of November, 1718, and reached Ocracoke Inlet on the 22d. Brand had timed his expedition well, for, as he had hoped, Thatch was at his rendezvous with his crew, which numbered, at this time, not more than twenty men. The pirate had received an intimation from Knight of the intended attack, but he had evidently treated the warning lightly, for he was wholly unprepared for a conflict when the Virginians hove in sight. It did not require many hours for him to make ready for action, however, and when the sloops came within range, having mounted eight guns, he gave them a broadside, which was a decided indication that the capture would be no easy one. In the course of the battle Thatch succeeded in boarding one of the attacking sloops, and although he had a reduced number of men, the Virginians were forced to a desperate resistance, and did not maintain one inch on their decks which was not dearly paid for in blood. Thatch himself attacked Maynard, with whom he maintained a bloody struggle, until a sword-cut across the throat, as he was in the act of emptying his pistol into the breast of the gallant officer, disabled him, and he was promptly dispatched. The Virginians had twelve men killed and twenty-two wounded.[1] Thatch displayed a most desperate courage in the conflict, and, according to Johnson, " stood his ground and fought with great fury till he had received five and twenty wounds and five of them by shot." More than half the pirate crew was killed, and several escaped by jumping overboard and swimming ashore.

From Ocracoke Inlet Brand sailed into Bath with nine prisoners, and on learning that the greater part of the cargo

---

Brand accompanied the expedition in person, but, following Spotswood, I think it perfectly safe to say that he did. The order from Eden on Knight regarding the pirates' effects was certainly given to Brand. See Letters, Vol. II., p. 318. Pollock also corroborates Spotswood. See N. C. Col. Rec., Vol. II., p. 319.

[1] Spotswood's Letters, Vol. II., p. 275.

of the French prize was still stored in the town, he demanded that Governor Eden should deliver it into his custody. Eden does not seem at this time to have questioned his right to seize the goods and gave him an order on Knight for their delivery.[1] At first the guilty secretary denied " with many asservations " that any part of the cargo was in his possession, but finding Brand determined, he confessed, and the goods were found concealed in his barn.[2] With Thatch's head suspended from the bowsprit, and the prisoners and the spoil safe in the hold, the Virginians then sailed back home in triumph.

In fitting out this expedition Governor Spotswood was compelled by the nature of the enterprise to observe the strictest secrecy. The officers of the men-of-war were the only persons he acquainted with his design, not even his Council being taken into his confidence.[3] In March of the following year (1719) he made a full report of the matter to the Council, which endorsed his action and ordered the prisoners tried for piracy. The Council was not precipitate in its course, however. They considered postponing action until every member could be present, but it was thought that all doubtful points could be just as well discussed before the court, and the trials were ordered to proceed immediately.[4] They were held at Williamsburgh, and four of the accused were condemned and afterwards hanged.[5]

---

[1] Spotswood's Letters, Vol. II., p. 318.

[2] N. C. Col. Rec., Vol. II., p. 344.

[3] Spotswood's Letters, Vol. II., p. 274.

[4] N. C. Col. Rec., Vol. II., p. 327.

[5] An attempt to secure some details of these trials from the Virginia Admiralty Court Records proved fruitless. The clerk writes: " The earlier records of this Court are in such a condition that I fear that I cannot give you the information asked for. I cannot even tell whether they go back as far as 1719; they are piled up in heaps in an upper room of the custom house building, and have been in that condition ever since the war. At the evacuation of Richmond in the Great Fire, a large quantity of papers and records of the United States Courts, as well as of the General

The trials are of public interest on account of the efforts made by the North Carolina friends of the pirates to establish their innocence.[1] It seems that when Thatch violated his first pardon, instead of prosecuting him, the North Carolina authorities applied to England for a second dispensation in his favor,[2] and the second pardon was on its way to the Province when Brand went on his expedition.[3] Spotswood showed, however, that his later crimes were committed subsequent to the date of this second pardon.[4] The North Carolina authorities strongly resented Brand's invasion of the Province, and denied Spotswood's right to send the expedition without their permission. The pirates, they claimed, could not be taken to Virginia for trial without a special warrant from the king.[5] Governor Spotswood had very little respect for North Carolina ideas of justice, however, and he not only hanged the convicted pirates, but proceeded to condemn the confiscated property in the courts. In this case the North Carolina officials again entered a vigorous protest, taking exception to the jurisdiction of the court, and demanding that the goods be returned to them for condemnation.[6] This point was promptly overruled, whereupon they threatened to bring suit in England against Captain Brand for trespassing on the possessions of the Lords Proprietors, and Governor Spotswood, in order to protect that officer in case of an adverse issue of such a prosecution,

---

Court of the State of Virginia, were totally destroyed. * * * In order to get at the information which you wish it would require a long and tedious search among a mass of dusty and dirty books and papers, with little show of success."

[1] N. C. Col. Rec., Vol. II., p. 327.

[2] The indulgence granted by the Act of Grace expired Jan. 5, 1718, a date prior to Thatch's recent outrages. See opinion on the Act by the Attorney-General of England, N. J. Archives, 1st Series, Vol. IV., p. 329 *et seq.*

[3] *Ibid.*

[4] Spotswood's Letters, Vol. II., p. 319.

[5] See Pollock's Letters in N. C. Col. Rec., Vol. II., pp. 318-20.

[6] Spotswood's Letters, Vol. II., p. 318.

had the proceeds of the sale of the goods sent to England, so as to be ready for the proper persons, should the higher courts reverse the decision of the Virginia tribunals.[1]

The evidence brought out on these trials showed that the North Carolina authorities had been guilty of a most disgraceful participation in the crimes committed by Thatch and his crew. When the pirate chief was killed, among the other papers found on his person was a letter from Knight containing a covert warning of the intended attack from Virginia, and also indicating Governor Eden's interest and friendship,[2] and no doubt was left that both of these officials had entered into a secret business copartnership with the notorious outlaw.

Knight was at this time one of the most prominent men in the colony, and Governor Spotswood, in his reports of the affair to Secretary of State Craggs, in referring to him, called particular attention to the fact of "how dark a part some of their Officers have acted, particularly one who enjoyed the post of Secretary, Chief Justice,[3] one of their Lords'p's Deputys, and Collector of the Customs, [who] held a private Correspondence with Thach, concealed a Robbery he committed in that province, and received and concealed a considerable part of the Cargo of this very ffrench Ship w'ch he knew Thach had no right to give, or he to receive." "But," he concluded, "it would be too tedious to relate how many favourers of Pirats there are in those parts, and even in this Colony, had they power equal to their Inclination."[4]

The chief evidence against Knight was secured from Basilica Hands, one of Thatch's men who had been with him off Charles Town the previous June. Hands was not at

---

[1] Spotswood's Letters, Vol. II., p. 318.

[2] Williamson's N. C., Vol. II. Proofs and Explanations Rr.

[3] Knight was Chief Justice for March term, 1718, only. See Hawks, Vol. II., p. 139. Martin says he acted during the absence of Chief Justice Gale.

[4] Spotswood's Letters, Vol. II., p. 319.

Ocracoke when Brand attacked the pirate, but was captured at Bath when Brand went into the port after Thatch's spoil. He had been shot and wounded in a wanton manner by Thatch a few days before, and doubtless a desire for revenge on the pirate crew had much to do with inducing him to turn king's evidence so promptly. He gave an account of how the French vessel had been seized off the Bermudas while bound home from Martinique, and how she had discharged her cargo at Bath, the collector sharing in the spoil. So serious were these charges, and supported as they were by the letter from Knight which was found in Thatch's possession, the Virginia authorities thought it their duty to advise the North Carolina government of the state of affairs which had thus been brought to light. The Vice-Admiralty Court officials were accordingly ordered to have copies of the testimony made and sent to Governor Eden.

Although Eden naturally was not inclined to give the matter a very thorough and unbiased investigation, especially as the charges came from the Virginia authorities, the accusation was too grave a one to be passed by without some official notice. The necessity of passing some judgment on it was also made much more imperative by the fact that Spotswood had sent a full account of the occurrences and the attendant circumstances to the English government, and also to Lord Carteret, one of the Carolina Proprietors, and further connivance of the North Carolina authorities would have been certain to attract the attention of the Proprietors, if not of the high officials of the English government itself. So in April, 1719, the Council of the Province was convened, and the matter laid before it. The Council very properly was not disposed to be hasty, and after hearing the charges, ordered that the papers in the case be served on Knight and that he be summoned to the next meeting to give his defense.[1]

---

[1] Council Journals, N. C. Colonial Records, Vol. II., pp. 329-330.

Pursuant to this summons, Knight came before the Council on May 27th. His letter to Thatch was produced and read, and his handwriting identified by comparison with other papers which he had penned.[1] On being called on for his defense, Knight submitted a lengthy remonstrance, denying the allegations contained in the testimony taken in the Virginia court, and explaining that the letter to Thatch had been written in accordance with the orders of Governor Eden. A young man named Edmund Chamberlaine, who resided with Knight, also filed an affidavit in his behalf. It is not related how long the Council deliberated over this weighty matter, but their conclusion can easily be surmised.

"This Board," says the entry in the Council journal, "haveing taken the whole into their Serious Consideration, and it appearing to them that the foure Evidences called by the Names of James Blake, Rich'd Stiles, James White, and Thomas Gates were actually no other than foure negroe Slaves,[2] and since Executed as in the Remonstrances is set forth, and that the other Evidences so far as it relate to the said Tobias Knight are false and malitious, and that he hath behaved himself in that and all other affairs wherein he hath been intrusted as becomes a good and faithful Officer, and thereupon it is the opinion of this Board that he is not guilty, and ought to be acquited of the s^d Crimes, and every one of them laid to his charge as afors^d."[3]

The evidence submitted by Knight in his own defense placed Eden in a most unenviable light, but after the shameful acquittal of the guilty Secretary it is not to be wondered at that no record is found of any proceedings against his equally culpable superior. But the charge which had been preferred against Governor Eden was by no means forgotten, and his complicity in Thatch's crimes has ever re-

---

[1] Council Journals, N. C. Colonial Records, Vol. II., pp. 343-4.

[2] "Though cunningly couched under the name of Christians."— Knight's Defense, N. C. Col. Rec., Vol. II., p. 345.

[3] Council Journals, N. C. Colonial Records, Vol. II., p. 349.

mained a blot upon his name. Nor did the better element in North Carolina in his own time fail to be sensible of the ignominy which attached to their government through his conduct. Some time after the occurrences above related, Edward Moseley, a prominent official of the Province, was arrested for forcibly possessing himself of certain records, and he declared with significant sarcasm that the Governor was quite able to effect the arrest of honest gentlemen, but was powerless when it came to apprehending outlawed pirates. Eden was so stung by this charge that he prosecuted Moseley for defamation of character.[1]

---

[1] N. C. Col. Rec., Vol. II., p. 359.

CHAPTER V.

North Carolina and Virginia had by no means the exclusive privilege of dealing with the pirates at this period. While Spotswood was ordering invasions of the North Carolina coast, and Thatch was pursuing his lawless career in the vicinity of Bath, South Carolina was passing through an ordeal never before experienced by an English colony in North America. Governor Johnson, though a man of no mean force, believed, above all things, in invoking the higher authorities whenever the occasion seemed to warrant it. Thatch had hardly gained the security of his North Carolina retreat after so boldly laying Charles Town under tribute, before a letter was speeding across the Atlantic to the British Board of Trade, acquainting it with the unheard-of outrage the infamous " Blackbeard " had perpetrated, and requesting the presence of one or more war vessels for the protection of the city and the adjacent coasts.[1] But, as usual, the petition was pigeon-holed, and the South Carolinians again found their grievances ignored by those from whom they had the right to demand protection.

The summer of 1718 had drifted on without further incident, however, until the autumn, when the products of the Province were being prepared for shipment, and the harbor was full of sail, ready to bear the valuable cargoes to the markets across the water. The pirates evidently knew something of the times and seasons of business in Carolina. Although they sailed boldly up and down the coast from one rendezvous to another, and were prepared to accomplish as much mischief as whim or interest might dictate, during the

---

[1] S. C. Hist. Soc. Coll., Vol. II., p. 257.

summer they gave little trouble to the few vessels that sailed with their cargoes of indifferent value between England and Charles Town. As soon as the autumn fell, however, they began to prepare for active operations, and during the months of September and October their career found its culmination in a series of exploits unparalleled in audacity since the days of the previous century, when the buccaneers in the West Indies, under the leadership of the infamous Henry Morgan, held the seas against the combined fleets of the then powerful kingdom of Spain.

In many respects Major Stede Bonnet was the most remarkable of all the notorious sea-robbers of this period. As an old biographer points out, he was the last man who could have been expected to have launched out upon such an abandoned and desperate career.[1] A man past the meridian of life, of good antecedents, possessed of wealth and of a considerable degree of education and refinement, as such accomplishments went in those rude times, there was every reason for him to remain at home and end his days in peace and honor. He had served with some distinction in the army of Barbadoes, had been honorably retired after attaining the rank of major, and was residing at Bridgetown, at peace with all the world and in good favor with the citizens of that thriving colony. Besides this, Bonnet had no knowledge of the sea, and, as will be seen, knew so little of the requirements of a sailor's life that his first experiences resulted only in disaster and misfortune.

Johnson, who seldom has a good word for a pirate under any circumstances, is inclined to pity rather than condemn Bonnet. "This humour of going a-pyrating," he says, "proceeded from a disorder in his mind, which had been but too visible in him some time before this wicked undertaking; and which is said to have been occasioned by some discomforts he found in a married state." Whatever may have been the source of his alleged mental disorder, there was

---

[1] Johnson, Vol. I., p. 91.

undoubtedly much well-planned method in his madness, as he soon afterwards showed in his exploits along the American coast.

It was early in the year 1717 that Bonnet put into execution his nefarious designs. Being a man of wealth, he had no difficulty in finding such a vessel and equipment as he desired; and one dark night, in company with a crew of seventy desperate men, he sailed across the Bridgetown bar in a sloop of 10 guns, which he had christened the Revenge, a name common in all pirate fleets at that time. Leaving the Barbadoes far to the south, he made directly for the Capes of Virginia, and stationed himself in that great highway of commerce. In a few days he had taken a number of merchant vessels, several of which he burned, after plundering them and sending the crews ashore.

After paying his respects to the commerce of New York and New England in rather an aggressive manner, Bonnet sailed for South Carolina, and came off the bar of Charles Town in August, 1717. Here he anchored, and set a watch for any vessels that might attempt to pass in or out of the port. He had not waited long before a sloop belonging to Barbadoes, Joseph Palmer, master, hove in sight, followed almost immediately by a New England brigantine, under the command of Thomas Porter. The brigantine he sent into Charles Town, after relieving her of all the valuables on board, and the sloop he retained for his own use, after dismissing the crew.

History does not relate what account of his adventure Captain Porter carried into Charles Town, but if any attempt was made to capture the daring freebooter, it proved futile, for the brigantine had scarcely made her way across the bar when Bonnet weighed anchor, set all sail, and shaped his course for the coast of North Carolina, where he could refit his vessel for another cruise. He took the Barbadoes sloop with him, and burned her soon after going into the coast. After refitting the Revenge, Bonnet again put to sea, but without any definite determination as to where his next cruise would be, and it was at this time that his troubles with his crew commenced.

The Revenge had not been out from Barbadoes many days before the men discovered his ignorance of nautical affairs, and this discovery engendered a contempt which soon began to display itself openly, and it was only by the influence of his superior courage that Bonnet prevented an open mutiny. The crew was kept quiet by means of determined threats and frequent punishments, and the Revenge was now steered for the Bay of Honduras, the great southern pirate rendezvous. Here he met Thatch, the famous " Blackbeard " of North Carolina, and the two entered upon a cruise together. They had not proceeded far before Thatch perceived that his companion knew nothing of seamanship, and deeming him an unsafe man to be in command of so fine a sloop as the Revenge, coolly deposed him. Placing Richards, one of his own officers, in charge, he took Bonnet on board of his own vessel, where he gave him a post of ease and security. Bonnet was naturally enraged at this proceeding and chafed under the restraint of his subordinate position, but he was powerless to wreak his revenge. Thatch was all-powerful, and had a desperate crew in sympathy with him, whose contempt of Bonnet was equaled only by their fear of the new commander. The first prize taken by Thatch's newly-organized squadron was the Adventure from Jamaica, whose master, David Herriot, was destined to play a tragic part in Bonnet's subsequent career.

Bonnet was in company with Thatch on several cruises, including the celebrated one off Charles Town harbor in June, 1718, after which he sailed in the same fleet to Topsail Inlet, N. C., where the company was disbanded. This was a stroke of excellent fortune of Bonnet, for he was then able to resume command of his own vessel and proceed to sea on his own responsibility. And just at this juncture a combination of circumstances made it possible for him to return to his lawless trade under the most favorable auspices possible.

As we have already learned, George I. had the year before

issued a proclamation of pardon to all pirates who would surrender within twelve months to any qualified officer of the king and take the oath of allegiance; and about the same time war broke out between Spain and the Triple Allies. Bonnet now saw his opportunity to pursue his career, at least for a time, under the color of law, and he was not slow to avail himself of it. Leaving the Revenge in command of a subordinate officer, he proceeded to Bath, where he surrendered to Governor Eden, took the oath and received a certificate of pardon. At the same time he procured a clearance for his vessel for the island of St. Thomas, announcing his intention of applying for a commission there to privateer against the Spaniards.[1]

Thus armed with proper clearance papers, and a pardon issued by a legally constituted authority in the name of his Majesty, Bonnet was prepared to continue his career of crime and bloodshed under better auspices than those enjoyed by any pirate since the time that Kidd sailed from England with the personal sanction of King William himself. Returning to Topsail Inlet, he rescued a number of sailors who had been marooned by Thatch on a desert island, and shipped them on the Revenge, under the pretense of taking them to St. Thomas.[2]

Having thus procured a good crew, he made all preparations to go to sea, but as he was on the point of weighing anchor, he learned from a market-boat that Thatch was at Ocracoke Inlet with a small company of men. Bonnet had never forgiven Thatch for deposing him from the command of the Revenge, and there were also many other scores against him which he was anxious to settle. By this time he had attained considerable proficiency in seamanship, and having by his good fighting qualities gained the confidence

---

[1] See Howell's State Trials, Vol. XV.

[2] Spotswood, speaking of this expedition, says that it was conducted by " Bonnet Thatch." He evidently confounded the two men. See Vol. II., p. 273.

of his men, he determined to have it out with his old ally. He accordingly set sail for Ocracoke, but he was a few hours too late. Thatch had sailed away, and learning that he had gone up the coast, Bonnet followed fast after him, but his quest was unsuccessful, and after cruising about for a few days he went into the Virginia coast. On this expedition Bonnet appointed David Herriot as sailing master of his sloop. Herriot joined Thatch when his vessel, the Adventure, was taken in the Bay of Honduras, and he now had became one of Bonnet's most valuable lieutenants.

Bonnet at this time seems to have feared the consequences of his acts if he were captured under his own name, and he therefore styled himself " Captain Thomas," by which name he was afterwards known to his crew. He also changed the name of his vessel, and, as if to defy the English authority to the utmost, called her the Royal James, in honor of the Chevalier de St. George, the son of James II., who was at that time on the Continent plotting against the throne.

Having thus prepared himself for the most desperate enterprises, Bonnet boldly announced his true intentions to the crew, and declared his determination to sail up the coast toward New England in search of booty. His announcement was a surprise to some of the men,[1] but no loud demurrers were entered. In those times there was little difference between a pirate and a privateer, and the sailor who shipped on a vessel of the latter class suffered few pangs of conscience when the exigencies of the occasion required him to fight under the black flag.

After committing several piracies on the Virginia coast, Bonnet sailed to Delaware Bay, taking several valuable merchantmen and terrorizing the whole coast, the inhabitants of which were unable to send any force against him. There seems to have been some little show of hostility at Port Lewis, for when he wished to put some prisoners ashore

---

[1] See testimony in Howell's State Trials, Vol. XV., where the trial of Bonnet and his crew is reported, pp. 1231-1302.

there, he first sent a savage message to the inhabitants, threatening to burn the town if his men were interfered with when they landed.

The only captures made by Bonnet in Delaware Bay in which we are interested are those of the sloop Francis, Captain Peter Manewaring, and the sloop Fortune, Captain Thomas Read. These captures were profitable ones, and, apparently satisfied with the results of this cruise, he proceeded to return to Cape Fear, bringing with him the two sloops and their cargoes. The voyage was uneventful, nothing of interest happening, except on one occasion when the Francis was sailing at too great a distance from the Royal James, Bonnet ordered her to stand nearer in or he would scuttle her with a broadside.[1] This threat kept both the prizes, which were manned by their own crews, near enough to the pirate to preclude all possibility of their escape.

The fleet arrived at Cape Fear in August, 1718, and Bonnet immediately set his men to overhauling and repairing the sloop for another cruise. The Royal James proved to be very leaky, and the pirates found they would be detained for a much longer time than they had anticipated. It is highly probable, however, that they would have been permitted to leave Cape Fear without molestation had they not, in their haste to supply themselves with building material, captured a small shallop, which they broke up and used in repairing the Royal James. Soon after this vessel was taken, it was noised abroad that a pirate was rendezvousing at Cape Fear, and in a few weeks the intelligence had traveled as far south as Charles Town, where the government, since the experience of the preceding June, was determined to expend its every energy to keep the freebooters off the coast. As we have already seen, Charles Town had suffered severely from the insolence of the pirates, and the people

---

[1] Testimony of James Killing, in Howell's State Trials, Vol. XV., p. 1253.

were naturally alarmed lest another descent should be made on the bar. The naval force of the Province was in a very weak condition at this time, no war-vessels being stationed anywhere on this part of the coast, and Governor Johnson was at a great loss to know how to rid himself of the threatened invasion.

But the man was not wanting to the occasion. Colonel William Rhett, a gentleman of fortune and distinction in the colony, who at this time occupied the post of Receiver-General of the Province, waited upon the Governor and asked permission to fit out two vessels against the pirate, who, rumor said, was in fighting trim with a sloop of 10 guns and a hardy crew of sixty men. Accordingly a commission was issued to Rhett, and he pressed into service two sloops, the Henry, Captain John Masters, and the Sea Nymph, Captain Fayrer Hall. The Henry, the largest vessel of the two, was fitted with 8 guns and seventy men, and was selected by Rhett as his flag-ship on the expedition. The Sea Nymph carried the same number of guns and sixty men.

On September 10th Colonel Rhett went on board the Henry, and the two vessels sailed across the harbor to Sullivan's Island, where the final preparations for the voyage to Cape Fear were completed. But just as he was about to weigh anchor the plan of his voyage was suddenly interrupted by a piece of startling intelligence. A small sloop, with one Cook in command, belonging to Antigua, came into port and reported that she had been overhauled and plundered by no less infamous a pirate than Charles Vane, who lay in front of the harbor with a brigantine of 12 guns and ninety men. Cook also reported that Vane had captured two other vessels bound for Charles Town, one a Barbadoes sloop, Captain Dill commanding, and the other a brigantine from the Guinea coast with a cargo of over ninety negroes. The negroes had been removed from the brigantine and placed on board of a sloop commanded by the pirate Yeates, which Vane had been using as a tender. Yeates, finding himself in charge of a good sloop with several guns, a crew of fifteen men and a valuable cargo, determined to part company with Vane. Accordingly he shipped his anchor at midnight and sailed away to the south. Vane discovered the treachery before many hours, and was soon in hot pursuit, but finding no traces of the fugitive, he had returned to Charles Town just in time to intercept four vessels bound out for London. Two of these escaped and continued their voyage, but the Neptune, Captain King, carrying 16 guns, and the Emperor, Captain Power, with 10 guns, were both taken with valuable cargoes.

Such was the account of Vane's depredations as brought in by Cook, and the news was certainly of sufficient gravity to startle the town and rouse the inhabitants to a high pitch of anxiety. But it could not have come at a more opportune time. Rhett's fleet was ready to sail at a moment's notice, and orders were immediately issued to him to abandon the Cape Fear expedition temporarily, and proceed without delay to meet this more pressing danger.

On September 15th Rhett crossed the bar, and having learned from Cook that Vane had intended going into an inlet to the south to repair his vessel, he stood down the coast for several leagues, scouring the rivers and creeks, but without success. Vane evidently feared that Cook's accounts would bring out a force against him, and he made off in safety long before Rhett got to sea. The latter spent several days in his search for the enemy, but finding no signs of him, and believing all danger from this quarter to be past, he proceeded to the execution of his original design, without returning to make a report to Governor Johnson.

In the meantime Charles Town had again been thrown into a state of agitation by the news of the landing of some pirates some distance to the south. This intelligence was brought by no other than one of the pirate crew, and when it was learned that such a character had arrived and requested an audience with the Governor, the people, remembering a similar embassy which had been sent in by Thatch some months previous, were seized with great consternation. It was soon learned, however, that the pirate's errand was a peaceful one. He informed Governor Johnson that Yeates, who had escaped from Vane, had put into North Edisto river with his cargo of negroes, and wished to know if pardon would be granted him and his crew if they came to the city, delivered up the negroes and took the oath of allegiance. An affirmative reply was returned, and shortly afterwards Yeates and his fifteen men came in with the negroes, delivered them to the authorities and received their certificates of pardon.[1]

Rhett sailed for Cape Fear about September 20th. He must have spent some time in exploring the coast for Vane as he sailed along, for it was not until the evening of the 26th that he sighted the great headland from which North Carolina's chief river derives it name. The mouth of the stream was obstructed by sand-bars which could not be crossed with safety without the assistance of an experienced pilot. The merchantmen of Charles Town did no trading with the North Carolina coast and knew little or nothing of its shoals and bars, and the pilot whose services Rhett had engaged seems to have had no knowledge whatever of the channel. The sloops had scarcely entered the mouth of the river when both ran aground, but not before they had sighted the topmasts of the pirate and his two prizes over a point of land some distance up the stream. Rhett could not get his vessels afloat until late in the night, and was therefore compelled to wait for dawn before making any hostile movement.

The pirates in the meantime were not idle. They knew that their position was not one of perfect security, and the sentinel who was posted to guard against sudden attack reported the appearance of Rhett's fleet immediately after it

---

[1] From scattered notices in various authorities it seems that the North Edisto below Charleston and its vicinity was in a small way quite a pirate rendezvous. See Minutes, Provincial Council of Pa., Vol. III., p. 42, for narrative of Richard Appleton et al., whose vessel was fitted from there.

crossed the bar. In the growing dusk it was impossible to distinguish whether or not they were merchantmen, and Bonnet, or Thomas, as he now called himself, manned three armed boats and sent them down to reconnoitre. They had not come within gunshot before they perceived with what manner of craft they had to deal, and hastening back to the Royal James, they reported the result of their observations.

Bonnet was not slow to realize that the break of day would bring on a fight that would be to the death. The government of South Carolina would not have sent an expedition such a distance against him unless it was equipped for desperate work, and he began preparations for the heaviest combat his lawless life had yet engaged him in. All night the crew, incited to constant vigilance and unceasing labor by alternate threats and promises, worked, clearing the decks, and making ready for action.

On board the Henry and the Sea Nymph no less active preparations were in progress. Rhett and his men knew that defeat would mean instant death at the hands of the infuriated outlaws, and they were determined to make use of every advantage that superior equipment would give them. When Bonnet's boats came down the river early in the evening, the South Carolinians anticipated an immediate attack, and fearing that the attempt might be renewed, they lay on their arms all night, maintaining the strictest watch to avoid a surprise.

All through the long hours the sounds of preparation could be heard from the pirate sloop, and the dawn of Saturday, September 27th, disclosed a scene of activity such as had never before been witnessed in those secluded waters. The crews of none of the vessels had slept during the night, and when the first glimpse of day shone in the east, both parties were ready to enter the fight at a moment's notice. The sun had barely risen above the headlands which command the entrance to the river when the South Carolinians, looking across the point of land behind which the pirates lay, saw the sails of the Royal James being run up the masts and heard the rattle of the chains as the anchors were hoisted to the deck. A minute later the pirate craft swung around before the breeze which was blowing straight from off the land, and with all sail set, came flying down the river past the place where the two sloops lay at anchor.

Bonnet's design was evident. He saw that his opponents outnumbered him two to one,, and he determined to resort to the favorite pirate method of defense, and maintain a running conflict, trusting to the chances of escape that would be afforded him could he reach the open sea. Rhett divined his purpose, and both sloops weighed anchor and made for him as he rounded the sheltering point of land. Taking a position on either quarter of the Royal James with a view to boarding, the Henry and the Sea Nymph bore down in such a direction as to force Bonnet to steer close to the shore. Rhett had planned this movement without any knowledge of the river, and it proved as disastrous to his own vessels as to that of the enemy. In a few minutes the Royal James was aground, and the attacking sloops, unable to come about with sufficient dispatch, ran into the same shoal water and were soon hard and fast on the sandy bottom of the channel. The Henry grounded within pistol-shot of the pirate, on the latter's bow, while the Sea Nymph, in her endeavor to cut off the flight, struck the bank so far ahead as to be completely out of range, and was of no service until five hours later when she floated off on the rising tide.

As soon as it was found impossible to get the Henry afloat, Colonel Rhett gave orders for a heavy fire to be opened, and the ten guns with which the sloop was manned began pouring their broadsides into the pirate, while the crew kept up a continual fire with small arms which did almost as much execution as the heavier fire from the deck. During this part of the fight the South Carolinians were at a tremendous disadvantage. When the Henry and the Royal James went aground, both careened in the same direction, so that the deck of the pirate was turned away from the Henry, while every foot of the latter's deck was mercilessly exposed. The heavy shot from the South Carolinians could only take effect on the hull of the pirate, while their own deck could be swept from end to end at every discharge. Lying in these positions, the two vessels maintained for five hours a continuous and bloody contest. The South Carolinians, though under the most trying conditions, conducted themselves with the most dauntless courage. Exposed as was their position, it seemed certain death to attempt to man the guns; but notwithstanding this, every man stood to his post without a thought of flinching, and the conflict was not permitted to languish for a single moment.

The pirates saw their advantage from the beginning and availed themselves of it in every possible way. For some time it seemed certain that the victory would be theirs, and in spite of the spirit displayed by Rhett and his men, Bonnet considered it but a matter of a few hours when the pirate ensign would triumph over the colors of the King. They " made a wiff in their bloody flag," says a contemporary account, " and beckoned with their hats in derision to our people to come on board them; which they only answered with cheerful huzzas and told them it would soon be their turn."[1]

Both sides were confident, but the pirates, who enjoyed such an advantage at the beginning of the conflict, had a desperate disappointment in store for them. The issue of the battle now depended on the tide; victory would without any doubt be with the party whose vessel was first afloat. For five hours the flood poured up the river, and it was late in

---

[1] This account of Rhett's expedition and of the subsequent occurrences is taken from a pamphlet written from Charles Town and published in London in 1719, entitled " Tryals of Major Stede Bonnet and Other Pirates." It gives a minute account of the circumstances of the capture, and furnishes a stenographic report of the trial and condemnation of the pirates. The account of these trials given by Howell, Vol. XV., is evidently largely taken from this pamphlet. Through the courtesy of Mr. Daniel Ravenel of Charleston, I have been enabled to make full extracts from this rare publication.

the day before it was high enough to lift the sloops from their stranded positions. The pirates understood the situation fully, and one can imagine the consternation which seized upon the crew of the Royal James when they saw the Henry slowly righting herself as the rising flood swept higher and higher around her bows. Many of the crew declared for an immediate surrender, but Bonnet refused to listen to such counsel. Under the stress of excitement, the courage which failed him so ignominiously at the last was roused to a desperate pitch. He swore he would fire the ship's magazine and send the entire crew to the bottom before he would submit, and, drawing his pistols, he threatened to scatter the deck with the brains of any man who would not resist to the last, should Rhett attempt to come on board.[1] Bonnet's rage did not avail, however. There were spirits in his crew as determined as he, who preferred to take the chances of a trial, or a pardon, than to brave the death that a further resistance would immediately incur, and surrender was determined upon.

While the pirates were angrily debating the course they should pursue, Rhett set his crew to work and temporarily repaired the damage sustained by the rigging; and assuring himself that the hull of the Henry was intact, he stood for the Royal James with the intention of boarding her promptly, if this should be necessary to force a surrender. At this juncture, however, a flag of truce was received, and after a few minutes' negotiations the Royal James surrendered unconditionally. On boarding her, Rhett, who had not known who was the pirate chief, was surprised to learn that his captive—Captain Thomas, as he was styled—was none other than the notorious Stede Bonnet, whose name was known along the coast of every colony from Jamaica to Newfoundland.

As the Henry had borne the brunt of the fight, her loss was far greater than that of her companion sloop. She had

---

[1] See testimony of Ignatius Pell, Howell, Vol. XV., p. 1271.

ten men killed and fourteen wounded, several of whom died
subsequently of their injuries. The Sea Nymph had two
killed and four wounded.[1] The pirates, in consequence of
their sheltered position, suffered much less severely. Seven
of the crew were killed and five wounded, two of whom
died soon afterwards.

---

[1] Judge Trott, in passing sentence upon Bonnet, stated that 18
South Carolinians had lost their lives in this expedition. There is
a tradition that Rhett was shot through the body, but his active
participation in the recapture of Bonnet three weeks later seems
to indicate this to be an error. See Rivers, p. 285.

CHAPTER VI.

When the struggle of the 27th was at an end, and Rhett examined his little fleet, he found that it had been much injured by the pirate guns and would require considerable repair before it could be trusted to stand the return voyage down the coast to Charles Town. He accordingly remained at Cape Fear for three days, and on September 30th, with the Fortune and the Francis and the pirate sloop as prizes, sailed for Charles Town, where he arrived on October 3d, " to the great joy of the whole Province."

Two days later Bonnet and his crew of over thirty men were landed, and delivered into the custody of Captain Nathaniel Partridge, the provost-marshal of the Province. Charles Town did not at this early period of her history boast a prison—although that by no means indicated a lack of crime in the colony—and the pirates were placed under a heavy military guard and confined in the public watchhouse. Major Bonnet, however, fared somewhat better. It was generally known that he was a gentleman by birth, and the officials were inclined to treat him with a degree of consideration not accorded to common criminals, but which was soon found to be indeed ill-advised. The confinement at the watch-house was very severe, and the authorities agreed to permit Bonnet to remain in the custody of the marshal, at the latter's residence, two sentinels being placed around the house every evening at sunset.[1] A few days later David Herriot, the sailing-master, and Ignatius Pell, the boatswain, of the Royal James, who had agreed to become evidence for the Crown, were also removed to the residence of the marshal.[2]

---

[1] Preface, Tryals of Major Stede Bonnet and other Pirates.
[2] Ibid.

What hitch there could have been in the law concerning the trial of pirates in Charles Town is not known, but on October 17th the Assembly, which was in session at the Parsonage House of St. Philip's Parish, passed "An Act for the more speedy and regular trial of pirates."[1] The preamble of this act set forth that " divers great disorders, wicked practices, treasons, murders, robberies, depredations, and confederacies, have been lately committed in and upon the seas by those called pirates," and that " the numbers of them are of late very much increased, and their insolencies [become] so great that unless some remedy be provided to suppress them, . . . trade and navigation into remote parts will very much suffer thereby." The act was very little more than a re-enactment of the statute of 28 Henry VIII., but it indicated a determination on the part of the government to use every endeavor to punish the pirates, and to go about it in a strictly legal manner.

When one considers the repeated and flagrant outrages which had been perpetrated upon the Province, and upon the port of Charles Town especially, by Bonnet and his fellows, it is hard to believe that these men could have found friends in the city; but to the shame of the people such a fact must be recorded. Friends they had, and friends strong enough and numerous enough to be of very effective force in thwarting the officers of the law in the discharge of their duty. The date set for the trials before the Vice-Admiralty Court was yet four weeks off, and this gave their sympathizers ample time in which to prepare plans for their release. Unfortunately there are no records existing which give an account of the disturbances made in Charles Town during this interval. We only know of them from passing references which we find in the history of the trials,[2] which has

---

[1] 3 S. C. Stats., p. 41. To this act were also attached two lists of names of citizens from which the grand and petit juries were to be drawn at the approaching session of the Vice-Admiralty Court.

[2] See Ass't Att'y Gen. Hepworth's speech to the jury. Howell, Vol. XV., pp. 1248-9.

been preserved in minute detail. The result of these disturbances we do know, however.

After terrorizing the good people of the city for several weeks, Bonnet's friends proceeded to try their influence and the influence of pirate gold on the sentinels who were posted about the marshal's house. Their efforts were thoroughly successful, and on the morning of October 25th, three days before the date set for the trial, the city was startled by the intelligence that Bonnet and Herriot had escaped during the previous night and had fled from the city for parts unknown. Ignatius Pell, who was still in custody, told an interesting story of how they had attempted to induce him to fly with them and how his superior virtue had withstood the temptation.[1] But Pell's story threw but little light on the real situation. The two chief desperadoes had escaped, but through whose instrumentality no one knew save those whose self-interest prompted them to be silent. Corruption was undoubtedly at the bottom of it, and although Captain Partridge's name is not connected with the treachery by any of the authorities, the fact that he was superseded a few days later by Thomas Conyers, indicates quite strongly that he knew more about the matter than the Governor thought was consistent with the honest discharge of duty.

But the manner of escape was now wholly a subordinate matter. The pressing necessity was to recapture Bonnet and Herriot before they could make their way to North Carolina, and enter again upon their career of crime. Governor Johnson, with his usual promptness, issued a proclamation offering a reward of £700 for the capture of the fugitives. "Hue and cry and expresses by land and water" were made throughout the Province, the coast being scoured both to the north and to the south in hopes of discovering them.

Bonnet, on effecting his escape, was joined by a number of his friends who had previously procured a boat, and to-

---

[1] Preface, Tryals of Major Stede Bonnet, etc.

gether they sailed northward along the coast. The weather was very unfavorable, however, and after contending with adverse winds for several days, they were forced to return to Sullivan's Island in order to procure supplies from Charles Town. They had scarcely landed on the island, which is just opposite the city and but a few miles distant, when word was brought to Johnson of their arrival. He immediately detailed the bold Rhett with a detachment of picked men to attack and, if possible, bring the pirates back to prison alive. Rhett sailed from Charles Town in the night, and after searching for several hours among the forests of low myrtle which covered the sand-hills on the upper end of the island, came upon Bonnet and his party. Rhett's men promptly opened fire, and Herriot was instantly killed, and a negro and an Indian belonging to the company severely wounded. Bonnet thereupon surrendered, and the next day, November 6th, Rhett returned to Charles Town with his prisoner, who was placed in safe confinement to await his trial.[1]

In the meantime, on October 28th, the Court of Vice-Admiralty had been convened at the house of Garrett Vanvelsin in Charles Town, and the men who had made such a desperate resistance at Cape Fear were put on trial for their lives. This court was one of the most remarkable that had ever been convened in the Province. Nicholas Trott, Judge in Vice-Admiralty, member of the Council and Chief Justice of the Province, presided, assisted by the following distinguished citizens, who, according to the law of that time, were not members of the bar: George Logan, Esq., Speaker of the Lower House of the Assembly and late member of the Council; Ralph Izard, Esq.; Colonel Alexander Paris, who played so important a part in the revolution of the succeeding year; Captain Philip Dawes, George Chicken, Benjamin De La Conseillere, Esq., who, later in life, held a high position in the judiciary of the Province;[2] William

---

[1] Preface, Tryals of Major Stede Bonnet, etc.
[2] 1 S. C. Stats., p. 439.

Cattle, Esq., Samuel Dean, Esq., Edward Brailsford, Merchant; John Croft, Gent.; Captain Arthur Loan, of the ship Mediterranean, and Captain John Watkinson, of the King William.[1]

After the reading of the commissions of the judges, the grand jury was sworn, and Judge Trott proceeded to deliver his charge regarding the cases of piracy which were about to be considered. This charge is an interesting and unique paper, giving a complete synopsis of the law against piracy and all kindred crimes. It is replete with quotations from, and references to, many of the most ancient English commentators, and evinces an erudition which would be considered remarkable at any period.[2]

The prosecution was conducted by Richard Allein, the Attorney-General of the Province, assisted by Thomas Hepworth. Both of these gentlemen were distinguished at the bar, and both rose to the position of Chief Justice in after years, Allein holding that post twice. He succeeded Judge Trott in 1719, and was again raised to this dignity in 1727.[3] After the usual preliminaries, two indictments were given out, and the grand jury returned true bills against the following for piracy committed on the sloops Francis and Fortune:

Stede Bonnet, Robert Tucker, Edward Robinson, Neal Patterson, William Scott, Job Bailey, John Brierly, Robert Boyd, Rowland Sharp, Jonathan Clarke, Thomas Gerrard, David Herriot, John William Smith, Thomas Carman, John Thomas, William Morrison, William Livers, Samuel Booth, William Hewett, John Levit, William Eddy, Alexander

---

[1] S. C. Adm. Court Records, Book A and B.

[2] Howell, State Trials, Vol. XV.

[3] The name of Thomas Hepworth does not appear as Chief Justice in the list given in the S. C. Stats. (Vol. I., p. 439). My authority here is the MS. Hist. of S. C. by General Edw. McCrady, which I consider the best existing authority on colonial history. Through the courtesy of the author I have been permitted to peruse several chapters of this work. Hepworth, according to him, was C. J. from 1724 to 1727, when Allein was again honored with the post.

Amand, George Ross, George Dunkin, Thomas Nicholls, John Ridge, Mathew King, Daniel Perry, Henry Virgin, James Robbins, James Mullet, Thomas Price, John Lopez, Zachariah Long, and James Wilson.

The case for the Crown was laid before the jury by the Attorney-General, who, in an address of some length, summed up the results of the late piratical operations of which the Carolina coast had been the scene. " If a stop be not put to these depredations, and our trade no better protected," he said, " not only Carolina, but all the English plantations in America will be totally ruined in a very short time."[1] He pointed out how Jamaica had already been ruined by pirates, reviewed the extraordinary circumstances connected with the visit of Thatch, and denounced " the most unheard-of impudence " of Richards, and Thatch's other messengers, who " walked upon the Bay[2] and in our public streets to and fro in the face of all the people," while awaiting the Council's reply to the pirate's demand for tribute. The exhibition of sympathy for Bonnet, whom he denounced as the " Archipirata," excited his peculiar abhorrence. " Who can think of it," he exclaimed, " when you see your fellow-townsmen, some dead, and others daily bleeding and dying before your eyes!"[3]

Hepworth followed Allein with a more detailed account of the disturbances which the friends of the pirates had caused in the city. " I believe you cannot forget," he said, " how long this town has labored under the fatigue of watching them, and what disturbances were lately made with a design to release them, and what arts and practices have lately been made use of and effected for the escape of Bonnet, their ringleader; the consideration of which shows how necessary it is that the law be speedily executed on them, to

---

[1] Howell's State Trials, Vol. XV., Trial of Bonnet et al., pp. 1243-44.

[2] East Bay street, commonly known as " the Bay," was then as now the street upon which all business connected with shipping was transacted, all the wharves running back to it from the water.

[3] Howell, Vol. XV., p. 1246.

the terror of others and for the security of our own lives, which we were apparently in danger of losing in the late disturbance when under a notion of the honour of Carolina they threatened to set the town on fire about our ears."[1]

The court then proceeded with the trial of all the accused, except Bonnet and Herriot, who were still at large. The testimony given by Pell, the boatswain, was not voluminous, but it was to the point. He detailed with great brevity the story of the capture of the sloops the Francis and the Fortune, and gave some evidence about the taking of five vessels off Charles Town by Thatch and Bonnet, in the capture of which all the accused had participated.[2]

The defendants were not represented by counsel. While the old law had long since been abrogated, the members of the South Carolina bar still deemed it " a base and vile thing to plead for money or reward,"[3] and it is not surprising that no one was found who would undertake the cause of the accused from feelings of personal interest. The prisoners made practically no defense, all of them claiming that they had been forced into piracy, but Judge Trott, in that arbitrary manner which brought him to grief a year later, cut short their protestations of innocence, and denounced them from the bench in a style that would justify one in thinking that he had been trained in the school of Jeffries during the days of his bloodiest assizes. All of the accused were found guilty except Gerrard, Sharp, Nichols and Clarke, and Judge Trott, in a lengthy discourse on the enormity of their crimes, sentenced them to death. The manuscript of this sentence is preserved in the Charleston Library and is one of the most unique documents of the colonial period now in existence. It is interspersed with innumerable Scripture references and quotations, and the annotations show a familiarity with both ancient and modern authorities rarely to be found even among jurists of acknowledged learning and ability.

---

[1] Howell, Vol. XV., pp. 1248-49. [2] *Ibid.*
[3] Fundamental Constitutions, LXX.

On November 8th, two days after Bonnet's recapture and return to prison, the condemned men were hanged at White Point, and their bodies buried in the marsh below the low-water mark. The exact spot of execution is not known at the present day, as the city has long since grown beyond the ancient low-tide marks, and old White Point, with its numerous creeks and desolate mud-flats, is now occupied by a populous and fashionable portion of Charleston. Tradition has it that the execution was held at a place now in Meeting street near the corner of Water, a few hundred yards below the historic St. Michael's Church, and nearly a quarter of a mile from the beautiful White Point Garden and the seaside promenade which now marks the southern boundary of the city.

Two days after the tragic scene at White Point, Stede Bonnet was arraigned at the bar to answer for his many crimes. The same judges and the same prosecuting attorneys were present in this case, which lasted through several days. Judge Trott, whose tyrannical conduct on the bench has become a part of South Carolina's history, made short shrift of Bonnet and his defense, but despite the overbearing attitude of the court, the old Barbadoes soldier, steeped to the lips as he was in vice and crime, maintained his dignity through it all, and while conducting himself with the greatest courtesy, declined to be browbeaten by either court or counsel.[1] When he was brought back to Charles Town and learned the fate of his companions he evidently abandoned all hope of escape, and attempted comparatively little defense, listening with perfect composure to the scathing denunciations of the Attorney-General, and the damaging charges of the court to the jury. He made no attempt to excuse himself for his flight from prison, but passed all references to it in silence.

To preclude any possibility of his escaping justice—for his friends were still active and were using every means to

---

[1] See Howell for Bonnet's defense.

secure his acquittal—the Attorney-General brought two separate indictments against Bonnet, to both of which he pleaded not guilty. The first trial was on the charge of taking the Francis, and after hearing the same testimony as was submitted in the trial of the crew, the jury rendered a prompt verdict of guilty. On the announcement of this decision Bonnet withdrew his plea in regard to the Fortune, and entering one of guilty, received the death sentence from Judge Trott. This sentence, which has also been preserved,[1] is on a par with the other papers which have been handed down from that learned jurist. He did not spare the prisoner in his denunciations, and for his benefit painted the horrors of eternal punishment in a frightful detail which would be considered barbarous and brutal in these more civilized times. "Consider," he said to the condemned culprit, "that death is not the only punishment due to murderers, for they are threatened to have their part in the lake which burneth with fire and brimstone, which is the second death,—Rev. 21. 8. See chapter 22. 15.—words which carry that terror with them, that considering your circumstances and your guilt, surely the sound of them must make you tremble, for who can dwell with everlasting burnings?—chap. 33. 14." After administering these comfortable words to the poor wretch, giving him, at the same time, his scriptural authorities with great scrupulousness, Trott informed him that all this was his duty to him "as a Christian." Before concluding, he reviewed in brief the prisoner's past life, the advantages of education and training he had enjoyed, and assigned what he considered the cause of Bonnet's downfall. "I have just reason to fear," he said, "that the principles of religion that had been instilled into you by your education have been at least corrupted, if not entirely defaced, by the skepticism and infidelity of this wicked age; and that what time you allowed for study was rather applied

---

[1] See "The Tryals of Major Stede Bonnet and the Pirates." Also Howell, Vol. XV., pp. 1298-1302.

to the polite literature and vain philosophy of the times than a serious searching after the law and will of God."

Trott having sentenced Bonnet to death, it remained with Governor Johnson to name the day of execution, and December 10th was selected. Although the prisoner had borne up under his sentence with great resolution, long before the fatal day arrived he resigned himself to a state of abject terror and agony that little comported with his firm attitude on the trial. It is said that so unnerved was he by the prospect of death "that he was scarce sensible when he came to the place of execution."[1] Despite the desperate character of the culprit, so pitiful was his behavior that the sympathies of the public were greatly aroused in his behalf, and much pressure was brought to bear on Governor Johnson to induce him to grant either a pardon or a commutation of his sentence. Bonnet himself was desirous of being carried to England so as to have his case brought directly to the attention of the king, and he wrote a letter to Colonel Rhett, imploring him to use his influence with the Governor to procure such a dispensation in his favor.[2] Colonel Rhett's reply is not preserved, but he is said to have taken such an interest in Bonnet as to offer to carry him to England,[3] and ample security was offered for the Major's safe delivery to the home authorities.[4] But Johnson knew what the Province had suffered at the hands of the pirates, and he would listen to no proposition to parley with them or their friends. He had no sympathy with the movement to procure a stay of Bonnet's execution, and was unswerving in his determination that the arch-pirate should die in accordance with the sentence of the court. It is possible that had he not made so desperate an effort to escape the government might have been induced to ameliorate his punishment, but he was considered too dangerous a criminal to deal with in any but the most relentless manner. Herriot, who had been killed on

---

[1] Johnson, Vol. II., p. 320.   [2] Ramsay, Vol. I., p. 204.

[3] Johnson, Vol. II., p. 320.   [4] *Ibid.*

Sullivan's Island, had been persuaded to renounce his old companionship and appear as king's evidence, and the fact that Bonnet had succeeded in again corrupting him was one that especially aroused the indignation of the officers of the law, and made them unyielding in their determination that Bonnet should have justice meted out to him, untempered with mercy.[1]

A piece of evidence which had been furnished by Captain Manewaring of the Francis, also had an undoubted influence with the Governor, as showing Bonnet's real feeling toward the Province. On the night before the battle at Cape Fear, while his men were busy preparing for the conflict, he addressed a letter to Governor Johnson, which he showed to Manewaring. This letter—which it is needless to say was never sent—was very insulting in its tone, and declared that if the sloops which had just appeared had been sent out against him, he would, in case he effected his escape, burn or otherwise destroy all vessels he could intercept coming in or going out of Charles Town.[2] To have shown mercy to such a man would have been a public crime, and Bonnet was hanged in accordance with his sentence, and his body buried with those of his companions in guilt, within the flowing of the sea which had witnessed so many of his dark and bloody crimes.

A few days before his execution he addressed a letter to Governor Johnson, in which he begged most piteously for mercy, pleading the ridiculous excuse that his crimes had been committed under compulsion. This letter was published by Captain Charles Johnson some years after his execution, and is worthy of reproduction, as it gives undoubted proof of the alleged facts of his education, although it indicates a pusillanimity and cowardice on the part of the once dashing officer in the presence of death which should have inspired feelings of complete disgust in the public mind of Charles Town, instead of arousing its sympathies as it did.

---

[1] Howell, Vol. XV., p. 1291.   [2] Johnson, Vol. I., pp. 98, 99.

The following is a copy of this remarkable letter:

" Honoured Sir:

" I Have presumed on the Confidence of your emminent Goodness to throw my self after this manner at your Feet, to implore you'll be graciously pleased to look upon me with tender Bowels of Pity and Compassion; and believe me to be the most miserable Man this Day breathing; That the Tears proceeding from my most sorrowful Soul may soften your Heart, and incline you to consider my dismal State, wholly, I must confess, unprepared to receive so soon the dreadful Execution you have been pleased to appoint me; and therefore beseach you to think me an Object of your Mercy.

" For God's Sake, good Sir, let the Oaths of three Christian Men weigh something with you, who are ready to depose, when you please to allow them the Liberty, the Compulsion I lay under in committing those Acts for which I am doomed to die.[1]

" I intreat you not to let me fall a Sacrifice to the Envy and ungodly Rage of some few Men, who, not being yet satisfied with Blood, feign to believe that if I had the Happiness of a longer Life in this World, I should still employ it in a wicked Manner, which to remove that, and all other Doubts with your Honour, I heartily beseech you'll permit me to live, and I'll voluntarily put it ever out of my Power by separating all my Limbs from my Body, only reserving the use of my Tongue to call continually on, and pray to the Lord, my God, and mourn all my Days in Sackcloth and Ashes to work out confident Hopes of my Salvation, at that great and dreadful Day when all righteous Souls shall receive their just rewards: And to render your Honour a further Assurance of my being incapable to prejudice any of my Fellow-Christians, if I was so wickedly bent, I humbly beg you will, (as a Punishment of my Sins for my poor

---

[1] There is no record to be found anywhere as to who these men were, or of why they did not appear on the trial.

Soul's Sake), indent me as a menial Servant to your Honour
and this Government during my Life, and send me up to the
farthest inland Garrison or Settlement in the Country, or in
any other ways you'll be pleased to dispose of me; and likewise that you'll receive the Willingness of my Friends to be
bound for my good Behaviour and constant Attendance to
your Commands.

" I once more beg for the Lord's Sake, dear Sir, that as
you are a Christian, you will be as charitable as to have
Mercy and Compassion on my miserable Soul, but too
newly awaked from an Habit of Sin to entertain so confident
Hopes and Assurances of its being received into the Arms
of my blessed Jesus, as is necessary to reconcile me to so
speedy a Death; wherefore as my Life, Blood, Reputation
of my Family, and future happy State lies entirely at your
Disposal, I implore you to consider me with a Christian
and charitable Heart, and determine mercifully of me that
I may ever acknowledge and esteem you next to God, my
Saviour; and oblige me ever to pray that our heavenly
Father will also forgive your Trespasses.

" Now the God of Peace, that brought again from the
Dead our Lord Jesus, that great Shepherd of the Sheep,
thro' the Blood of the everlasting Covenant, make you per-
fect in every good Work to do his Will, working in you
that which is well pleasing in his Sight, through Jesus Christ,
to whom be Glory forever and ever,[1] is the hearty Prayer of
" Your Honour's
" Most miserable, and
" Afflicted Servant,
" Stede Bonnet."

---

[1] Hebrews xiii. 20-21.

CHAPTER VII.

The month of October, 1718, was one of turmoil and excitement in Charles Town. There had been rioting by night, threats of burning the town, and intimidation of the officers of the law, and the government was almost powerless to preserve the safety of the citizens of the Province. The town-watch, which had been established but a few years, was still in an imperfect state of organization, and disorders were not easily quelled. The militia guard around the public watch-house proved sufficiently strong to prevent Bonnet's crew from being released, but, as has been seen, the guards at the house of Marshal Partridge, where the leader was held in custody, were not proof against bribery, and three days before the time set for the trial, the country had been thrown into a state of alarm by the intelligence of the escape of Bonnet and his chief officer. Rumors were abroad concerning the descent of combined pirate fleets upon the coast, and a sense of the most imminent danger was realized, not only by the government, but by every citizen of the Province. They felt that their homes and their families were not safe. The pirates in times past had not scrupled to put the unprotected cities of the Spanish dominions to the torch for purposes of revenge, and they were now exhibiting a spirit of audacity not equaled by their most daring leaders since the days of Morgan's rule in Jamaica. The Carolina coast was wholly unprotected, the recent Indian wars had exhausted the fighting strength of the military, and a pirate force could have sailed up the harbor, and landed in front of the custom-house before a single movement could have been made to oppose it.

Nor was this sense of danger on the part of the Carolinians a newly-awakened one. Numerous petitions had been sent to England by the government, as well as by private citizens, praying for assistance and relief,[1] but the home government had its hands full of its own affairs and nothing was done to aid the colony. These conditions had now been existing for many months, and so serious had the situation become that long before the pirates had commenced their serious outrages, addresses from the Representatives and inhabitants had been presented to the authorities by Joseph Boone, the London agent of the colony, relating their miserable condition, arraigning the Lords Proprietors for neglecting their duty, and praying that " their once flourishing Province " might be added to those already under the jurisdiction of his Majesty.[2] But these applications, urgent as they were, received no attention, and matters grew worse and worse until now it seemed that the colony was to be destroyed by the hand of its lawless enemies.

On the capture of Bonnet, Governor Johnson addressed an appeal to the Lords of Trade, giving a faithful account of the recent happenings, and expressing the fear that the pirates infesting the coast would be so enraged at the capture, that the colony, as well as its trade, would be greatly endangered. He represented to the Board the necessity of immediate protection, and begged that a war-vessel be stationed at Charles Town without delay.[3]

This communication was dated from Charles Town, October 21st, 1718, and the ink was scarcely dry on its pages before the Governor's worst fears were realized. Bonnet was still languishing in prison awaiting trial when news was brought that one Moody, a notorious pirate, was off the bar with a vessel carrying 50 guns and 200 men, and that he had already taken two vessels bound from New England to

---

[1] S. C. Hist. Soc. Coll., Vol. II., p. 235.

[2] *Ibid.* Also Vol. I., p. 249.

[3] S. C. Hist. Soc. Coll., Vol. II., p. 237. This letter was delayed, not being received until the following May.

Charles Town.[1] Governor Johnson, immediately on the receipt of this intelligence, convened his Council and laid the situation before it. He represented to the members the danger of invasion, and the hopelessness of expecting aid from England. The colony, impoverished as it was, must strike a final blow in its own defense, and for it to be certain, the blow must be swift. His proposal was that an armed fleet be sent out against the invader without the loss of an hour's time. The Council, which was composed of the oldest and most experienced men in the Province, was well acquainted with the past history of the pirates on their coasts, and did not fail to appreciate the gravity of the situation, and the wisdom of the Governor's advice. After consultation, it was unanimously decided to adopt his suggestion, and preparations were immediately entered upon to equip an armament of sufficient weight of metal to cope with the 50 guns which Moody could at any moment bring to bear upon the illy-equipped forts around the city.

At this time there were nearly a score of trading vessels in the harbor, and to them the government turned for aid. But it was not to be expected that a sea-captain who had no personal interest in the port or its people would volunteer to run his vessel into so great danger where the hope of reward was so slight, and it was therefore found necessary to press the required ships into this extraordinary service. After making an examination into the condition of the available shipping, the Council selected the Mediterranean, Arthur Loan, master; the King William, John Watkinson, master;[2] and the Sea Nymph, Fayrer Hall, master, for the perilous expedition. To this fleeet was added the Royal James, Bonnet's old vessel, which was being held in Charles

---

[1] The account that follows here is taken partly from the S. C. Adm. Court Records (Book A and B), and partly from a letter written to Johnson by a person residing in Charles Town at the time. (Hist. of Pyrates, Vol. II., p. 324).

[2] Loan and Watkinson will be recognized as two of the assistant judges in the Bonnet trials which were being held at this time.

Town as a prize. She was placed in command of Captain John Masters, former master of the Henry, Rhett's flag-ship in the Cape Fear expedition. Eight guns were mounted between her decks, and the old pirate craft was, for once in her lifetime, fitted out for honest work. The Mediterranean was mounted with twenty-four guns, the King William with thirty, and the Sea Nymph with six. Having secured the necessary fleet, the Council apprehended some difficulty in finding a sufficient complement of men, and Governor Johnson issued a proclamation calling for volunteers, and promising them all the booty that might be taken.

On Rhett's return from Cape Fear, he had had a quarrel with Johnson in consequence of some action of his in connection with that expedition, and the Governor determined to take command of this enterprise and lead the fleet against the pirates in person at the earliest possible moment.[1] This action infused confidence into the people, and in a few days three hundred volunteers were on board the vessels awaiting orders to sail. But a serious delay was still to be met. The masters of the impressed vessels made no objection to giving their personal services to the colony, but their owners were to be considered, and they now entered a formal protest, strongly representing that some security should be given by the government to indemnify them for the possible injury or capture of their vessels by the pirates. Governor Johnson recognized the justice of their plea, and immediately convened an extra session of the Assembly and laid the case before it. Without delay the Assembly voted a bill to secure the ship-owners against all losses and expenses they might incur.

---

[1] This reason for Rhett not joining the expedition is based on a letter of the Proprietors on the subject, which censured him for certain action connected with the Cape Fear expedition. This letter was never sent, however, and the Proprietors thanked him for the part he played. See Rivers, p. 285. At the same time, however, they held him highly culpable for not assisting Johnson in the present instance. See S. C. Hist. Soc. Coll., Vol. I., p. 168.

These proceedings delayed the expedition for about a week, but in the meantime scout-boats had been stationed along the shore of the islands at the harbor entrance, with orders to resist any attempt on the part of the enemy to land, and at the same time an embargo was laid on all shipping. Several days before the fleet was ready for sea, the boats off Sullivan's Island sighted a ship and a sloop, which, coming up to the bar, dropped anchor and attempted to land. They were prevented by the guards, however, who made a hostile demonstration on their approach, and for three days the two strange craft lay quietly at their moorings, making no movement calculated to arouse further suspicions.

Late on the evening of November 4th the fleet sailed down the harbor, and anchored several hundred yards below Fort Johnson, which commanded the main entrance to the port.[1] Orders had been issued for every movement to be made with the least demonstration possible, and the vessels reached their anchorage without being detected by the enemy. They lay quiet all night, and as the gray mist of early morning crept slowly over the ocean, Governor Johnson, from the deck of his flag-ship, the Mediterranean, signaled his consorts to weigh anchor and follow him. The commander of each vessel had been carefully instructed before the fleet had left Charles Town. No warlike display was to be made until the final moment, and the four vessels now steered in the direction of the pirate fleet with the guns all under cover, and the men below decks. By eight o'clock they were close to the enemy. The deception was complete. Mistaking them for merchantmen, the pirates promptly weighed anchor, and stood in toward the mouth of the harbor to intercept the retreat which they were certain would be attempted. Having placed themselves between the South Carolinians and the harbor, they now hoisted the black flag

---

[1] See allegations of Loan *et al.*, in libel against N. Y. Revenge, S. C. Adm. Court Rec., Book A and B.

and called on the King William to surrender.[1] At this moment Johnson ran the king's colors to the masthead of the Mediterranean, threw open his ports and delivered a broadside which swept the decks of the nearest vessel with murderous effect. Before they had recovered from the consternation into which they were thrown by this sudden manœuvre, the South Carolinians bore down upon them, and began the battle in desperate earnest and at the closest possible quarters. The hatches were thrown open, the men poured from below the decks, heavily armed, while the 68 guns of the combined fleet poured broadside after broadside into the pirates, who were now hemmed in between the shore and the open sea. By skillful management, however, the ship escaped from this precarious position, and made all sail possible in order to elude the desperate chase of the South Carolinians. Johnson signaled the Sea Nymph and the Royal James, or the Revenge, as she was now called, to look to the sloop, while he, in company with the King William, made hot pursuit after the ship, which seemed to have every chance of escape.

The pirate sloop, which carried six guns and 40 men, unable to reach the open sea, was now vigorously attacked by Hall and Masters. The pirates defended themselves with a valor worthy of a better cause, and for four hours, with the vessels almost yard-arm to yard-arm, they maintained the fiercest struggle ever known in those waters. Finally they were forced to abandon their guns and seek shelter in the hold from the tremendous fire which was sweeping the vessel from stem to stern. A few moments later the South Carolinians came alongside and boarded, despite the desperate resistance made by the captain and the few men who had not fled below. Reaching the decks, the attacking party made quick work of the pirates, although the latter defended themselves with the desperation of men who real-

---

[1] Arthur Loan *et al. vs.* the Eagle. S. C. Adm. Court Rec., Book A and B.

ized that they had but one chance left to them for life. In a short time every man above decks, including the chief, who fought to the death with the fury of a lion, was either killed or disabled, and the boarding party found itself in undisputed possession of the vessel. The men who had fled into the hold surrendered without another blow, and a few hours later the sloop, with her surviving crew fast in irons, was carried into Charles Town in triumph. The struggle, which took place almost within sight of the city, created the most tremendous excitement among the inhabitants, which rose to a pitch of almost indescribable exultation as the throng along the wharves saw the Sea Nymph and the Revenge rounding into the harbor, the royal ensign at the masthead signaling their victory.

Governor Johnson, while not forced to such desperate fighting as his subordinates of the Revenge and the Sea Nymph, had a long, hard chase after the fleeing ship, and did not come up with her until the middle of the afternoon. During the pursuit the pirate abandoned the defense and bent every energy to effect his escape. He lightened the ship in every possible way, and even threw over the guns and boats, but all to no avail. The South Carolinians had the fastest sailers, and as soon as they came within range, Governor Johnson ordered the King William to open fire. The first discharge raked the deck of the ship, killing two of the crew, " and having received a shot between wind and water," the pirates hauled down the black flag and made an unconditional surrender.[1]

When the hatches were opened, to the great surprise of the captors it was discovered that the hold of the ship was crowded with women, and, upon investigation, the vessel proved to be the Eagle, bound from London to Virginia and Maryland with one hundred and six convicts and " covenant servants," whom it was designed to settle in those colo-

---

[1] Arthur Loan *et al. vs.* the Eagle. S. C. Adm. Court Rec., Book A and B.

nies, thirty-six of them being women.[1] The Eagle had been captured by the pirate sloop, which was known as the New York Revenge, near Cape Henry, and converted into a tender. Six guns had been placed in her, and her name was changed to the New York Revenge's Revenge, John Cole being given the command. A large number of the crew and of the convicts allied themselves to the pirates, while those who refused to join them were held as prisoners.

A still more serious surprise awaited the Governor, however, on his return to Charles Town to look after the issue of the conflict between the sloop and the rest of his fleet. It was ascertained that the captured vessels did not belong to Moody at all, nor did the captive crews have any connection whatever with him. The commander of the pirates, who had been killed on board the sloop, proved to be no less notorious a personage than Richard Worley, who had so terrorized the coasts in the vicinity of New York and Philadelphia but a few weeks previous. Naturally Johnson was much gratified at having exterminated so dangerous a company of outlaws, but the question as to the whereabouts of Moody was still one of vital interest to the colony. The statements of the prisoners were certainly not above suspicion, and no one could say positively that Worley's crew was not a part of Moody's company. It was altogether possible, if not probable, that Moody was hovering within the headlands of one of the neighboring harbors, and would, if in his power, wreak a cruel revenge on the colony for the capture and slaughter of his confrères.

To guard against the possibility of his making a sudden descent on the port, Johnson determined to maintain his fleet in a state of thorough organization until he was satisfied that all danger was past. A few days afterwards the public anxiety was relieved by the arrival of the Minerva, Captain Smyter, from the Madeira Isles. Smyter reported

---

[1] S. C. Adm. Court Record, Book A and B, inventory of the Eagle's cargo.

that he had been taken off the bar by Moody, who about the same time received information of the preparations which were being made in Charles Town to capture him. He had accordingly taken the Minerva about a hundred leagues out to sea, where he had plundered her, after which he set sail for New Providence in order to avail himself of the king's proclamation of pardon, which had been brought out by Governor Woodes Rogers.[1]

Worley's career as a pirate was a brief, though remarkable, one, his exploits extending over a period of less than six weeks. He set out from New York during the latter part of September, 1718, in an open boat, with eight companions. They ran down to Delaware Bay, where they plundered a small vessel, which, upon being released, went to Philadelphia and reported the outrage. The news created much alarm, and advices were sent to New York warning that government of the danger. An expedition was fitted out against Worley,[2] but proved unsuccessful, and a few days later he captured a Philadelphia sloop, which he converted to his own use. His ravages were so continual during the next few weeks that the Governor of Pennsylvania ordered his Majesty's war-ship Phoenix, which lay at Sandy Hook, to go in quest of the desperadoes. The Phoenix scoured the coast, while Worley stood out to sea, and thus he escaped the second time. He then made his way south, and arrived off Charles Town just after Moody had taken flight, and, knowing nothing of the preparations in progress, he fell a victim to the fate that Governor Johnson had prepared for the other, but not less dangerous, enemy.[3]

The majority of the prisoners brought into Charles Town on this occasion had been dangerously wounded, and the authorities made all haste to have them condemned and

[1] Johnson, Vol. II., p. 239.

[2] Minutes Provincial Council Pa., Vol. III., p. 49.

[3] Johnson, Vol. I., p. 342 *et seq.*

executed lest they should die of their injuries before the law could be vindicated. Accordingly, on November 19th, Judge Trott convened the Vice-Admiralty Court at the house of Garrett Vanvelsin, and twenty-four indictments were given out by the Attorney-General, fifteen being based on the circumstances of the taking of the Eagle, near Cape Henry, and nine on those of the capture of the Expedition on October 29th, near Hatteras. The trials lasted for five days, and a verdict of guilty having been returned in every case, Judge Trott, on November 24th, passed sentence of death upon the entire company. Pursuant to this sentence the following men were executed a few days later: John Cole, commander of the Eagle, " alias the New York Revenge's Revenge "; Thomas Prizgar, John James, Abraham Henderson, Ralph Mudge, John Swinnock, William Queen, William Ford, Nicholas Whealan, Sabastien Taunten, Daniel Stannel, John Clarke, Thomas Shaddock, and Francis Frisher, John Borfield, John White, Nathaniel Cade, William Vaughn, John Mason, John Ryley, George Pocock, John Acon, Richard Jackett, and James Lincolne. The last nine, together with Cole, belonged to the New York Revenge's Revenge, or the Eagle, and were convicted on evidence implicating them in the capture of the Expedition. During these trials, Andrew Allen, a prominent merchant and shipowner of Charles Town, whose vessel, the Providence, had been captured by pirates two years before, sat on the grand jury.

Dr. Alexander Hewat, the old colonial historian of South Carolina, is guilty of a serious error in regard to the Worley expedition and trials which has caused every subsequent writer to go astray. He states that the pirate crew " fought like furies until they were all killed or wounded except Worley and another man, who even then refused to surrender until they were likewise dangerously wounded. These two men, together with their sloop, the Governor brought into Charles Town, where they were instantly tried, condemned and executed to prevent their dying of their wounds."[1]   Dr. David Ramsey, who in a large part of his history follows Hewat blindly, often using him *verbatim et literatim* without according him the slightest credit, repeats the error,[2] and Professor Rivers, who is usually very painstaking and accurate, has permitted himself to be led off into the same misstatement.[3]   These writers could easily have found the correct account of the conflict and the subsequent proceedings by referring to the Vice-Admiralty Court records, which are contemporaneous, and are as full on many of the points as any historian could wish.   Johnson, in his "History of the Pyrates," committed the same error, although he corrected it in a later edition.   It is not improbable that it was on Johnson's earlier edition that Hewat based his account.   It is rather a remarkable circumstance that although the Admiralty Court journals have been freely accessible for a hundred years or more, and contain much material of the greatest value, they have been wholly neglected, and have been used in no single case that can be found.   It is hardly probable that their existence has all the time been unknown.

While much has been preserved regarding the exploits of Worley and his capture by Johnson, unfortunately the records of the trials of the pirates who survived, are very meager, and but little testimony can be gathered from them. In the subsequent proceedings looking to the condemnation of the prizes, the claim of Edmond Robinson, chief mate of the Eagle, gives in an interesting and unique manner the details of the capture of that vessel by the pirates.[4]   He says:

" On the 24th Day of October last past being in about the Latitude of Thirty Seven Degrees North, and Thirty Five Leagues distant from Cape Henry, met with a certain Pyrate

---

[1] See Carroll, Vol. I., p. 210.

[2] Hist. of S. C., Vol. I., p. 203.

[3] Early History, p. 285. The error is also repeated in Winsor, Vol. V., p. 324.

[4] S. C. Adm. Ct. Rec., Book A and B.

Sloop, named the New York's Revenge, Commanded by one Richard Worley, a Pyrate since Dec'd who Chased the said Ship Eagle Galley all that Day, and fired a volley of small arms at them, and kept them Company all that night, and the next Day being the Twenty fifth of the said October, the said Pyrates hoisted a black Flagg with a humane Skelleton on it which so much terrified the Said Ship Eagle's Company, that the men not only refused to fight, but also hindered the Officers themselves in their Duty of Defending the said Ship Eagle Galley, and many of them ran into the hold whereupon the Said Pyrate Crew came up along side the Said Eagle Galley, and swore that if the Eagle's Company would not strike their pennant, they would kill every soul of them, which was done. . . That the said Pyrates having as aforesaid gotten possession of the Said Ship Eagle Galley barbourisly beated the Said Staples and Severall of his men for being so bold as to fire at them, and then forced the Said Staples and all the others into the Said Pyrate Sloop. . . And the Said Pyrate afterwards called the Said Ship Eagle Galley by the Name of the New York Revenge's Revenge, and put one James Cole, a Pyrate, to Command her as Captain thereof, together with other Pyrates. That the Said Pyrates having New named the said Ship Eagle Galley, and named her as aforesaid, came and lay off the Barr of Charlestown."

In the operations against the pirates the colony had so far been victorious. Two of the most dangerous freebooters on the coast had been taken and hanged, together with their crews, but the danger was by no means past. The sea was yet covered with pirate craft, manned by as desperate outlaws as any of those who had paid the penalty of their crimes at White Point. Every month brought intelligence of renewed outrages, of vessels sacked on the high seas, burned with their cargo, or seized and converted to the nefarious uses of the outlaws.

Governor Johnson was no dreamer, and he did not lull himself into a fancied security because of the success of the exploits of the daring Rhett and himself. South Carolina had on more than one occasion before felt the vengeance of the pirate hordes, and he knew that every effort would be made to visit it on the impoverished colony again; and should the blow fall, his judgment told him that it would come with a more crushing force than ever before. The Province itself was unable to do anything more. ²The cost of the two naval expeditions had wrecked the already depleted treasury, and as yet the English authorities had given no indication of their intention to do anything to assist their hard-pressed fellow-countrymen in the distant colony.

But Johnson did not despair, although he did not encourage the thought of expecting any assistance from abroad. On the contrary, he insisted that the people should help themselves, and in February, 1719, the Assembly passed an act appropriating sufficient funds to pay the debts incurred by the equipment of the two expeditions.¹ In the meantime the Governor had forwarded another letter to the Lords of Trade, in which he gave a full account of the recent occurrences, narrating how his fears had been realized, and insisting that a ship-of-war should be sent to South Carolina immediately unless their Lordships were willing to see the trade completely ruined. In this communication the Governor expressed himself with great earnestness, claiming for the colony some consideration at the hands of the Board, and reminding it that during the previous year the Province had supplied for the use of his Majesty's navy 32,000 barrels of tar, 20,643 barrels of pitch, and 473 barrels of turpentine.²

---

¹ 3 S. C. Statutes, p. 69. Gov. Johnson in a letter to the Board of Trade claimed to have expended £1000 from his private purse in forwarding these expeditions and otherwise assisting the Province during these troublous times. See S. C. Hist. Soc. Coll., Vol. II., p. 239.

² S. C. Hist. Soc. Coll., Vol. II., p. 236. In hopes of destroying the Swedish monopoly, the government was at this time offering a bounty on naval stores sent from the colonies. See Cunningham's Growth of Eng. Industry and Commerce in Modern Times, p. 285.

If the principle that great bodies move slowly were applied in the present case, it would prove the British Board of Trade to have been the most ponderous body in all the complex organism of the English government. The last-mentioned communication, which was written on December 12th, 1718, was received on February 24th, 1719, and the urgency of the case must certainly have been appreciated at a glance. But the imminent danger which was threatening one of the finest Proprietaries of the Crown, situated in a remote and unknown region a thousand leagues beyond the sea, was not a matter of sufficient import to disturb the distinguished repose of these noble Lords, and two months passed before they would even so much as deign to have the communication read in their counsels. Having finally received a formal reading, Mr. Secretary Craggs, to whom it was referred, considered it, and consented to recommend to the Lords of the Admiralty that the request for a ship-of-war be granted. This recommendation was adopted with a qualification, and the whole matter was referred back to the Board of Trade, and at last, on April 29th, a letter was forwarded to Governor Johnson, acknowledging the receipt of his last communication, stating through what circuitous channels his application had passed, and informing him that the Lords of the Admiralty had consented to send a frigate " as soon as possible."[1]

While Governor Johnson was busying himself seeking relief from England, the courts of the Province found themselves engaged with an immense amount of litigation growing out of the pirate captures, which sunk the government still deeper in debt. While the men who went out with Rhett and Johnson to do battle with the public enemy were, in many cases, actuated by the highest motives of patriotism, they were not wholly uninfluenced by the hope of substantial reward.[2] It is not surprising, then, that the courts were

---

[1] S. C. Hist. Soc. Coll., Vol. II., p. 258.

[2] See S. C. Hist. Soc. Coll., Vol. I., p. 195, for notice of payment of bounty from the Crown to the captors of the Royal James, etc.

overwhelmed with condemnation proceedings instituted by the men who had undertaken the enterprises. There were claims and counter-claims, and the court records of the time are filled with depositions and decrees in cases, the costs of which must have amounted to a greater sum than the value of all the property involved in the voluminous litigation.

Bonnet was yet languishing in prison awaiting execution when John Masters and Fayrer Hall, commanders of the sloops Henry and Sea Nymph respectively, entered a libel suit in the court of Vice-Admiralty against the Royal James, alleging the manner of her capture, and praying the court to order "all and singular the Negroes, Goods and Merchandise aboard the same" to be condemned and sold and the proceeds turned over to the captors. Colonel Rhett, who seemed to be the only one on the Cape Fear expedition who did not demand a reward for his services, waived all claim to any part of the Royal James as a prize. Attorney-General Allein, acting in the capacity of a private attorney, appeared for the libellants, and, after a lengthy trial, Judge Trott appointed Rhett agent for the court, and decreed that the prizes should be sold and the proceeds given to the captors. Several parties had entered claims to portions of the cargo, alleging that they had been dispossessed of it in an unlawful and piratical manner by Bonnet. These claimants were allowed one-half the value of their property.

The result of Master's connection with Governor Johnson's expedition was another suit in Admiralty, in which he was joined by Captains Loan, Watkinson, and Hall, all of whom were anxious to be paid in full for the services they had rendered the Province. Of all this group of cases, the one which attracted the most interest was that against the Eagle, which, as we have seen, was rechristened the New York Revenge's Revenge when taken by the pirates. All the officers, and that portion of the crew which had refused to join the pirates, were in Charles Town, although the commander, Robert Staples, who had been so "barbourisly beated" by Worley's men, had died before the trials were begun. Edmond Robinson, the chief mate, had assumed command of the crew, however, and engaging legal counsel, he made a hard fight in behalf of his owners for the vessel and her cargo. The fact that Governor Johnson had promised all prizes to the volunteers was a point on which the libellants fought with much determination. But what gave the case its great interest was the peculiar nature of the cargo. It was a unique sight, even in that day, to see litigants wrangling over the actual possession of something more than a hundred white slaves,—for such they were to all intents and purposes. Judge Trott, after hearing a voluminous mass of testimony and argument, decreed that the "convicts and covenant servants" should be "publickly sold, or assigned over to such persons as shall be minded to purchase them for the several terms" for which they were bound or sentenced, the proceeds, less the expenses of sale, to be delivered to Robinson as agent for his owners. History relates nothing concerning the sale of these human chattels, which was certainly one of the most remarkable ever known in the annals of slavery in America.[1]

---

[1] The foregoing is all based on the MS. Vice-Admiralty Court Records, Book A and B.

CHAPTER VIII.

The events of the autumn of the year 1718 can be said to have forever ended the exploits of the pirates on the Carolina coasts   Not that they were entirely exterminated, but seeing the desperation of the South Carolinians, they concluded that it was wiser to be discreet than valorous, and shifted the scene of their operations.   Here and there we find accounts of further outrages, but these were only isolated cases, and had no effect on the commercial life of the Province.   Occasionally a pirate would be captured and brought into Charles Town, and while no records of any further trials are extant, there is reason to believe that executions took place later than 1718.

The colonists had the pirates on the run, and whenever they appeared on the coast it was only to remain for a short period, secure what booty they could, and make off in hot haste before the authorities could learn of their presence. In the summer or early autumn of 1719 the inhabitants were still further relieved by the arrival of the man-of-war Flamborough, Captain Hildesley, which was placed on duty at Charles Town, while the Phoenix, Captain Pierce, which had made an unsuccessful attempt to capture Worley, cruised along the coast, keeping a sharp eye out for any of the freebooters who might venture to depredate on the commerce of any of the colonies.[1]

In December, 1719, the South Carolinians, despairing of prosperity under the Proprietary government, broke out in

---

[1] Hewat, in Carroll, Vol. I., p. 249. The Boston News Letter of July 16th, 1724, says that 130 pirates were captured off Charles Town, and that each of the captors received £5000 as his share of prize money. This is an absurd exaggeration.

open revolt, and declared James Moore Governor in the name of the King. Johnson, who was very popular, was offered the government on the condition that he would renounce the authority of the Proprietors. This he declined to do, and was driven from power. A few months later, Moore was superseded by Governor Francis Nicholson, late of the Province of New York, who, upon his accession, found the Province entirely freed of the fear of the pirates. Shortly before the late revolution, news was received at Charles Town of an intended attack by the Spaniards of Havanna, and the Province was thrown into a state of agitation lest the pirates should ally themselves with the enemy, and seize the opportunity to wreak their vengeance on the colony. So startling was this intelligence that the Flamborough was immediately dispatched to New Providence to intercept the invaders from that point, but a storm scattered the Spanish fleet, and the vessel returned to Charles Town with the pleasing information that danger was past.

When Governor Nicholson arrived, the colonists had so far recouped themselves that they could with ease have beaten off the pirates had they made their appearance. They were still considered such a dangerous menace, however, that Nicholson received special instructions regarding them. He was told what was to be done with them and their effects in the event of their capture, and his attention was particularly directed to the English statutes on the subject.[1] Having assumed the reins of government, he immediately communicated with the home authorities regarding the appointment of a commission to hear all cases of piracy, and an order of Council was issued creating such a body.[2]

There seems to have been some controversy as to who should constitute the commission. Governor Nicholson submitted his nominees, and Colonel John Barnwell and

---

[1] See instructions to Nicholson, S. C. Hist. Soc. Coll., Vol. II., p. 145.

[2] Sept. 20th, 1720. S. C. Hist. Soc. Coll., Vol. II., p. 149.

Mr. Joseph Boone, the London Carolina agent, also suggested a number of persons for the positions.[1] The final nominations were made by the Council to the Board of Trade, and before the end of the year the new regime was ready to proceed with all cases in proper legal form.

Nicholson occupied the governorship until 1725. During his administration no trials were held, although had the war-vessel stationed at Charles Town kept proper watch the good people of the Province might have feasted their eyes on more than one more tragic scene at White Point. On numerous occasions the Charles Town merchants were given great unrest by rumors of pirates in the vicinity of the port, and a number of outrages went unavenged. The first was in the summer of 1722, when George Lowther, the famous English freebooter, appeared off the coast. He had been off the bar several days when the ship Amy, commanded by Captain Gwatkins, came out of Charles Town, bound for England. Lowther attacked him immediately, running up the usual "bloody" ensign and ordering a surrender. Gwatkins, so far from being terrified, returned the pirate's fire, and attempted to close in for a fight at close quarters. Lowther had not calculated upon such a movement and sought to escape, but the Amy crowded him so close in to the shore that his vessel went aground, and the crew was forced to save itself by swimming ashore. Gwatkins, unwilling to leave the pirate to right his vessel and continue his cruise, tried to set fire to the stranded bark, and while engaged in the attempt was fired upon from the beach and killed. The Amy's men retreated to their vessel and continued their voyage, while Lowther got his sloop afloat and put into an inlet on the North Carolina coast for repairs. He spent the winter in North Carolina, and continued his cruise again in the spring of 1723.[2]

The next outrages during Nicholson's administration

---

[1] S. C. Hist. Soc. Coll., Vol. II., p. 149.
[2] Johnson, Vol. I., pp. 361, 362.

were perpetrated by the New England freebooter, Edward Low, whose desperate exploits were the wonder of his time. In company with Harris, a desperado whose career was scarcely less infamous, Low came to the South Carolina coast in May, 1723, and in the course of a very short time captured the Crown, Captain Lovereigne, the King William, Captain Carteret, and a brigantine, all of which had just come out of the harbor of Charles Town. Having plundered these vessels, he shortly afterwards took the Amsterdam Merchant, Captain Williard, in the same vicinity. This vessel was from Jamaica and was owned in New England, and as a special mark of his regard for his old home he cut off Williard's ears and slit his nose before dismissing him. No record of the exact number of vessels taken by Low on this cruise has been preserved, but it is known that a few weeks later he seized two brigantines bound from Carolina to London, and a schooner bound from New York to Carolina.

These captures do not seem to have caused any great agitation in Charles Town, and it is probable that no news of them was received until some time after Low had left the coast. About a month later Low and Harris were attacked by the war-ship Greyhound, and the latter captured with all his crew. They were carried into Rhode Island and condemned for piracy, and hanged near Newport.

Despite these interruptions, the commerce of Carolina prospered during this period as it had never done before since the founding of the colony. The people made great strides along all lines of development, and when Nicholson returned to England in 1725, leaving Arthur Middleton in control of affairs, the colony was one of the most valuable attached to the Crown. Francis Yonge, the London agent, had little to do save to submit gratifying reports of the state of trade, and if there were any piratical incursions during the latter years of his term, they produced so slight an effect on the great current of business that they were not considered worthy of any official notice.

There are few notices of the pirates from 1723 to 1730. William Fly, who was executed in Boston shortly afterwards, took the sloop John and Hannah on the North Carolina coast in 1726,[1] and one Lewis, during this period, spent several months in North Carolina trading with the people, during which residence he managed to evade the vigilance of the officers of the law.[2]

In 1730 Robert Johnson, who had been deposed from the governorship in the revolution of 1719, was again raised to that dignity. Some idea can be gained of how the pirates of his former administration had been forgotten when we learn that in his commission he was given no authority to proceed against criminals of this class, and his instructions contained only a more or less perfunctory clause in regard to them.[3]

For more than four years after Johnson's resumption of office, the Province was undisturbed by even so much as a rumor of pirates, but in August, 1734, there was evidently some apprehension on the part of the government that the properly constituted commission might be needed. Shortly before this time a Spanish schooner, the crew of which had mutinied and killed the master, was brought into Charles Town, and the circumstances were such that Johnson had one of the sailors arrested for piracy. The commission for the trial of pirates in Carolina had expired on the death of George I. in 1727, and there was so little use for it that the new sovereign had never renewed it. He had issued a proclamation, however, that all officers be continued at their posts until further advice. On the strength of this the Governor ordered the case heard before the old commission, and forwarded a record of the trials to the High Court of Admiralty in England for approval.[4]

---

[1] Johnson, Vol. II., p. 232 *et seq.*   [2] *Ibid.*, p. 254.
[3] S. C. Hist. Soc. Coll., Vol. II., p. 179.
[4] S. C. Hist. Soc. Coll., Vol. II., p. 263. On Nov. 6th, 1728, judges were commissioned in all the colonies to try pirates. See N. J. Archives, 1st Series, Vol. V., p. 196. It seems that the commissions for Carolina, though regularly issued, were never sent to the Province.

Just what the other cases of this period were is not known, but it is certain that they were several in number.[1] In communicating an account of his course to the Duke of Newcastle, Johnson asked for the issuance of a new commission, and it not being granted, he did not deem it of enough importance to warrant his pressing the application.

By this time the pirates on the coasts had been completely exterminated, and vessels came and went, unarmed and unguarded, without fear of interruption. Eight years afterwards, in 1742, Lieutenant-Governor Bull, in announcing the death of Vice-Admiralty Judge William Trewin, incidentally called the attention of the Duke of Newcastle to the fact that no other commission for the trial of pirates existed than the one authorized by his late Majesty, and prayed that a new one be issued.[2] The request was the second time ignored, and was never renewed. The reason for the existence of the commission no longer held good; the pirates who had once terrorized the country and paralyzed the chief branches of trade were no more, and the commission, lately so important a part of the governmental economy, was now only a useless appendage which could well be permitted to expire.

Although the pirates themselves were seen no more along the coast, they had made too deep an impress on the history of the Carolinas to be forgotten, and for many years, here and there in the statutes, an obsolete clause regarding the method of trial and punishment stands out like an ominous warning from the past. As late as 1736 an act " For ascertaining public officers' fees " includes two heads, providing for the fees of the Register and Marshal of the Admiralty Court " for the tryal of pyrates." For drawing the death warrant of the condemned the Register was to receive two shillings sixpence, and for executing the extreme penalty of the law the Marshal was paid one pound.[3] In the days of

---

[1] S. C. Hist. Soc. Coll., Vol. II., p. 263.

[2] *Ibid.*, pp. 275-6.

[3] S. C. Stats., pp. 420-421.

Bonnet and Thatch, when the rabble of Charles Town was regaled with the ghastly sight of scores of dead men hanging from as many gibbets, the stout-hearted marshals drove a thriving trade, but times had now changed. Better days had come, and the grave colonial statesmen who still formulated laws against the ancient enemy with all the solemn usage of the English Parliament, did so knowing that they were but perpetuating a memory of the dark past,—of a period when the colony was driven through a fiery ordeal, which was survived only by the exercise of an indomitable courage, prompted by an abiding faith in the destiny which was to be realized in the future.

White Point. the "Execution Dock" of old Charles Town, still remains. Its desolate mud-flats have been converted into smiling gardens, surrounding stately old mansions, whose broad, colonnaded verandas and antique architecture carry one back to another century. Its extreme point, reaching out into the bay, is no longer a spot of superstitious dread, but, with its shady walks, offers a delightful retreat from the heat of the burning southern sun. Fort Johnson, whose guns were mounted nearly two hundred years ago to repel the invading enemy, is still seen across the harbor, and Shute's Folly, with its dismantled fortress of more modern times, stretches its low, marshy shore in front of the city, but little changed since the days of West and Morton, when its only ornament was a lofty gallows, from which pirates were hanged in chains until their blackened corpses fell to pieces beneath the action of wind and sun.